EGGSHELLS

Bryan Clover

Published by New Generation Publishing in 2019

First Edition

ISBN

        Paperback 978-1-78955-820-3
        Hardback 978-1-78955-821-0

www.newgeneration-publishing.com

 New Generation Publishing

Our daughter Evie died on 11th January 2018 from a highly aggressive brain tumour. This book wouldn't exist if she was still alive, so it is dedicated to the beautiful girl that we miss so much. Her own book "Written by the Stars" was the inspiration for me to start writing to ease through the pain of her loss. Both books can be bought through the website of Evie's Gift, the Charity set up in her name.

PROLOGUE

"Take another breath, Evie." That's the thought that was in my head the moment I watched Evie die. If you think you've felt stress and pain before, then it will probably have been nothing like this. We had been at home for six weeks since leaving the Bristol Royal Hospital for Children. Evie was in bed in our dining room, her head bandaged to keep the tumour at bay, unconscious for the last 24 hours from the level of morphine that had been administered to keep her pain-free. The previous few days had been hell. We had been desperate to delay the moment that we knew was coming. The inevitable that was so close. Tears … many, many tears. In-depth discussions with the oncologist about when to bandage her head, how much of a dose of morphine and other drugs she would need to be completely unaware of what was happening to her. The thought of her knowing that she was going to die was agonising. During her time in intensive care in Spain, the surgeons had removed a large section of her skull to allow the brain and tumour to expand outside her head and so relieve the intra-cranial pressure. Now the tension on her skin was untenable and a rupture would have been unbearable for her, for us. Infections, pain. We had spent the last 13 weeks utterly focused on Evie, her treatment, and her quality of life. We had forgotten about ourselves and were in no way ready for what was about to happen to us.

There isn't a Haynes Manual to tell you how to cope with the death of your child. Nobody has taken the time to write 'Being a Bereaved Parent for Dummies'. I don't think it is possible to write such a book. The first Europeans to explore the unknown of the New World had it easy compared to dealing with the death of a child. At least they had the stars to guide them. Losing Evie at 13 years old was so alien to us that we were staggered at how 'unknown' it felt. In those early months I felt completely and utterly lost: there is no other word for it. I wasn't 'numb' or 'in shock'. I was lost, pure and simple. For 13 years I had poured my love into this wonderful girl and now she was gone. Parents are not designed to outlive their children. It is fundamentally wrong on every level. Some parents rage at God for being so callous, but I just felt marooned, with no hope of rescue.

Anyone that has taken a wellness or mindfulness course will tell you that we base our decisions on how to cope with issues on the experiences that we have had during our lives. Each time we come across something where a decision is required, we look back at our lives for similar experiences to guide us, and aim to repeat what worked last time. But the loss of our child was so utterly different from anything else that none of our previous experiences worked. I lost my father in 2001 to cancer; we lost both of my wife, Patsy's parents within five days of each other in 2014, one to a heart attack, the other to a brain haemorrhage. Despite these experiences, when Evie died from a brain tumour, we were woefully ill-equipped to deal with it. It all happened so fast, we hardly had time to think. Thirteen weeks from her first headache to her death. The blink of an eye.

This book isn't designed to be a 'this is what worked for me, so give it a go' book. It isn't a 'self-help' book either. It is nothing more than me writing down what happened: how we crashed into mourning for our beautiful girl, and what we learned along the way. It will offer as many questions as answers, but above all it is here to show that (if you are reading this as a newly-bereaved parent) you aren't alone, however much it may feel like it. It will then lead into a short series of 'Wednesday Wisdom' pieces that I wrote for 'The Compassionate Friends' Facebook page, and these were then added to the Evie's Gift Facebook page as I felt that they had a message that others could benefit from. (We set up the Charity Evie's Gift within a few weeks of Evie's death to provide badly-needed help to parents whose children were critically ill in hospital far from home, as we had been in Spain). The Wednesday Wisdoms were a way for me to explore what was happening in my head and try to understand it all.

The book is a reflection of very personal and painful events, and how they affected me and to some degree, Patsy, my wife. Losing our daughter at the age of 13 was devastating and has changed us forever. This book isn't a joint view. It is just me. I will refer to Patsy sometimes, but that story is her's to tell if she wants to. It is not for me to reflect it here. We have each reacted to Evie's death in very different ways; part of my coping strategy has turned out to be writing. Patsy calls it a 'splurge' of information. In some sense, she is right: the outpouring of pain comes in an uncoordinated way, things jump around, but to me it doesn't matter. It's down on paper and that's all that counts. Writing it down helps me to understand, to reflect, and to think. As I write each chapter here, or each Wednesday Wisdom, I explore what I am saying and develop the different ideas further. Importantly, I always try to be honest with myself, because to do otherwise yields no benefit. Whether or not I will continue to write in the future is anyone's guess. Maybe, maybe not. I'm not even 100% sure that I will publish this book. I can't say that I have got pleasure out of writing this, but it most definitely has helped me to understand what is happening, and to some degree why. It has forced me to take a long hard look at myself and the person that I was, and that I am now; at what I have become. They are very different people. Getting the words out of my head is truly cathartic. It goes so much further than just thinking about something; my brain digs and explores as I write, it takes the next step in a thought process that doesn't happen unless I am writing or talking about it. There is less going around in circles.

There are parts of this story that are going to be painful or unpleasant to read. There will be times when you can sense my anger, frustration, or even self-pity. You may even feel a twinge of guilt if you recognise some of the moans about friends and acquaintances, but losing a child isn't a nice subject, so I make no apologies for the content or the emotion. If you are worried that some of the things that you have said or done might fit with what I am talking about, that doesn't matter. Talk to us. As you will see later on, changing behaviour is important. We all make mistakes, so just learn and correct them. If you've held back from talking about Evie, then talk to us. If you've not put Evie's name on a Christmas card because you didn't know what to do, then put 'EvieAngel' next time. We all have to learn, and sometimes it can be a slow process. You may also note contradictions, inconsistencies or changes in viewpoint, especially in the Wednesday Wisdoms. These simply reflect the changing nature of grief and how emotions can be so volatile over time. They are what they are. They are honest. I didn't write this to be a grammatically-perfect book, editorially-correct, I wrote it to help me heal.

I'm not going to pull any punches in the book, though. There's no happy ending, or enlightenment. Losing a child at 13 is a shitty thing to live through, so at times it doesn't make pleasant reading. Make no mistake, I have discovered that some people are amazing friends, some are outright cowards, and others are complete shits. There are two people out there who I wouldn't piss on if they were on fire, I'm that angry at them. Some are in the middle, floundering, and need us to guide them. I can count on the fingers of one hand the people that I can be totally honest with, but you know what, that's enough. Some people have said that I expect too much from others. Perhaps, but allow me to enlighten you: losing a child is a life-changing experience, it rips deep into your soul and there are days when the pain and darkness are so overpowering that many bereaved parents consider joining their children. A week after Evie died, I was experiencing constant headaches, and as Evie had died from a brain tumour, my GP wasn't taking any chances so sent me for a CT scan. The result came back clear; I was disappointed. I'd had enough of life and didn't want to be here. Those feelings change your perspective on everything. If we are to survive, we have to make radical decisions and choices. Before you judge me, try walking in my shoes for a while. The risk of suicide is very real for bereaved parents, myself included.

If you have lost a child yourself, then I hope that you can see from what follows in these pages that you aren't alone, and you certainly aren't going mad. What you are going through is 'normal'. All the confusion, emptiness, the exhaustion: it's all normal for what you are experiencing. People have been losing children for millennia, yet as a society we are absolutely rubbish at talking about it or even knowing how to help. Around 3,500 children under 18 die in the UK each year. I don't think that the way our society deals with it has anything to do with a stiff upper lip, I think it is more to do with our society becoming more introverted and selfish. Social media allows us to hide from others more easily. Gone are the days of talking over a garden fence; we live in the age of a text or Insta post. A virtual 'hug' just isn't the same.

It's an unknown world for all of us, but there is help and guidance out there – you just have to look for it. Importantly, you have to know where to go looking. Thousands of parents go through this every year, whether they lose a baby, a young child, a teenager, or an adult child. The pain doesn't lessen just because your son or daughter was 45 when they died. They are still your world, no matter how old they were. And the rest of the world is blissfully unaware of the agony that you are going through. Am I feeling sorry for myself? You bet I am. The world has lost an amazing young woman, my daughter, and I think that I am entitled to feel sorry for myself. I watch the news and see some of the utter bastards that are still walking this earth and I feel rage. The whole thing is criminally unfair. Why did God choose to take Evie? Don't worry, I'm not going to get bogged down in theology or religious rhetoric, as that could be another book in its own right.

Finally, in various places in the book I have used the word 'muggles' to describe people who have not lost a child. Obviously, it is nothing to do with non-wizarding folk, but just refers to those of you that have not experienced this type of loss; the phrase seemed appropriate as losing a child makes you feel completely different from everyone else.

Chapter 1

Our World Unravels

I suppose before I do anything else, I need to put the book into context; give a little background information. Patsy and I met at school, aged just 12. Like all boys at that age, I was pretty mean to her. We had our first date at 15, were engaged at 18, and got married at 23. Evie was born when we were 40. Up until a year or so before her birth, we had been in great jobs earning great money and enjoyed everything that life gave us. We had never been that interested in having a family. I 'retired' from the RAF at 38 and joined the charity sector. Then we decided it was time to have a child. It wasn't quite that clean a decision though. We spent a year trying to conceive, but because neither of us was young any more, it was a little more tricky.

I was driving back from London one evening after a wine tasting with Richard, a friend of mine, and he said to me, "I think the reason that you and Patsy don't have kids is that she wants them, but thinks that you don't, so she doesn't mention it." I told him he was wrong. The next morning, I told Patsy about the conversation and she stayed silent. We talked about it and both realised that we had both made completely the wrong assumption about what the other wanted. I owe Richard a huge debt for that moment of honesty, because it resulted in our amazing daughter. Having Evie was the most incredible experience, and I adored being a dad. I literally found my calling.

My side of the family is dominated by boys, so we naturally assumed that we would have a boy, even though we both wanted a girl. We decided not to find out what sex the baby was when the nurses offered. At 00:26, on Friday 24 September 2004, Evie Melissa Grace Clover popped into our world, weighing in at a healthy 8lb 3oz, and we were absolutely delighted. At that moment in time, I was the happiest man on the planet.

Both Patsy and I had been single-minded people: strong-willed and determined. We joked during her pregnancy that if Evie had our single-mindedness stacked on top of the other, we were going to be in for an interesting ride. She did. As she grew, Evie became completely happy in her own skin; she didn't care one hoot what anyone else thought, she never followed fashion, and did exactly what suited her. I was so proud of her for that. It took great strength of character to stand against the tide of fashion and peer pressure. Pink was still her favourite colour no matter how uncool it was. She made us smile.

Compared to some of the horror stories that we heard from other parents, Evie was a piece of cake to bring up. Patsy and I set our life goal as preparing her for adulthood, giving her the tools and skills that she would need to be a considerate, helpful human being who might just make a good contribution to society. We wanted to show her as much of the world as we could, and give her the confidence to try anything once.

As Evie grew, it became obvious that she was talented academically as well as being a natural swimmer. She loved school and learning, she excelled at mathematics (even though she didn't actually enjoy it), found science fascinating, and played the saxophone. She also represented her county at U15 Table Tennis, despite only being 12 years old. Evie could out-think Patsy and I. Whenever we played Cluedo, I lost, and Evie won most of the games, with Patsy fighting hard not to give in. Her young brain was working on a different level to ours. It thought faster. It was like the difference between a dial-up internet connection and fibre optic broadband. Evie loved food and ate voraciously. She tried anything that I put in front of her. Her favourite meal was steak, chips, and carrots. We once took her to a bistro near Bordeaux, and when the waiter asked her what she wanted, she asked for the steak that was on the specials board, and she wanted it 'à point', or pink. The waiter explained to her that the French version was very pink, well, nearly raw actually. She told him that was okay – she was ten. He looked at us, we nodded. The steak arrived and Evie demolished it, mopping up the excess blood with her chips. The waiter grinned from ear to ear. This girl knew what she liked.

Evie's academic prowess was proven when she won an academic scholarship to the Royal High School Bath, and I have a photo on my phone of her first day there, with her looking so pleased to be going to senior school. Evie had been relatively shy as a toddler and only two girls from her junior school went to the High School, so we had expected her to be nervous and not a little lonely. Not a chance. She grasped the opportunity with both hands and went for it. At her first parents' evening the following March, **every** teacher we saw used one word – 'amazing'. Strangely, we always had the devil of a job to get her to do her homework as she always took it to the wire. Likewise, she was always reluctant to practice her saxophone, but somehow managed to do enough to progress each week. She loved dinosaurs and was thrilled by space and the planets. She made the best Victoria sponge I have ever eaten. It was always light and fabulous.

I was so proud of Evie in so many ways. When she died I crashed through the floor. Evie was growing into a wonderful, caring young woman. She would have made a fabulous doctor or teacher, she cared so much about others. Fundamentally, Evie was a very happy child. She loved school and learning, had a great bunch of friends, and was growing in confidence. Evie was truly unique and never followed the crowd.

Our 'journey' started at 0620 am on Thursday, 12 October 2017, when Evie came into our bedroom and told us that she had a headache and felt sick. She vomited, and in classic Evie-style, immediately asked for breakfast. School rules stated that we had to keep her off school for 48 hours following any bout of sickness, so we did, even though she was outwardly fine. On Sunday we had a repetition of Thursday, but this time we sent her to school on Monday as we were rapidly approaching half term and didn't want her to miss too much. Again, outwardly she was fine. As the week progressed, she was very tired and felt sick most days, but after a 30-minute lie down in the nurse's room she was a bit better. By Thursday morning on the 19th October, she couldn't shake whatever it was that was making her feel ill, so we took her to the doctor. They carried out a number of neurological tests, which didn't reveal anything significant, and put it down to period-related migraines or cluster headaches. We were due to drive to Plymouth at the weekend to catch a ferry to northern Spain for a two-week, half-term break, so the doctor reckoned that a holiday and some sunshine would do her good.

On the Sunday night ferry to Santander, I was grumpy with Evie at dinner because she wasn't eating. Looking back, I feel terrible about what I said to her when I told her off. I should have known that for Evie to turn down food, something must be very wrong. Why didn't I spot it? Why didn't I realise that she was ill? But I didn't, I just got irritable with her. Of course, even if I had spotted it, it wouldn't have changed anything, and there was little that we could have done on the ferry anyway. Now, I feel terrible about that, knowing the pain that she must have been experiencing. I have been to her grave and apologised to her, and asked for her forgiveness, but I still feel pretty shitty about it. I should have known better.

That night on the boat, Evie had a really rough time of it, more migraines, sickness, and discomfort, which continued through the Monday until we arrived at our apartment in San Sebastian around 5 pm. For days we had been dosing her up with ibuprofen and paracetamol, but it wasn't getting close to getting rid of the pain. Evie went to bed pretty much as soon as we arrived in the apartment, got up for dinner, was sick again, then went back to bed. By mid-evening she was being sick again and finally at 2:30 am enough was enough, so we took her to A&E.

Dealing with the medical world in San Sebastian was an interesting experience. We were in a foreign country where the first language was Basque, not Spanish – all x's and k's. We had to rely on Google translate to get our message across to the nurses in A&E. Within 5 minutes she'd been examined by a nurse, within 20 minutes Evie had seen the on-call doctor, and not long after that the on-call neurology team arrived. The NHS could learn some serious lessons here: none of your five-hour waits just to be triaged, all at about three o'clock in the morning. How many UK hospitals have on-call neurology teams at 3 am? They didn't like what they saw, so they admitted her.

As soon as the CT scan teams were in, they sent Evie for a scan, and by ten o'clock our world imploded when they showed us the image of a massive brain tumour sat right in the midline region of her brain. It was the size of a clenched fist. We had gone from having a normal little holiday to fighting for Evie's life in no time flat. Having admitted her to the children's ward, by lunchtime they decided to send her to the paediatric intensive care unit (PICU) as they wanted to monitor her more closely. By late afternoon one pupil had dilated, and they were sufficiently worried about her inter-cranial pressure that she underwent emergency surgery to remove about 30% of the bulk of the tumour. She returned to PICU with a drain fitted in the early hours of the following morning. We were in pieces, but relieved that she had survived the surgery. Later that day the surgeons decided to remove a section of her skull to allow the brain and tumour to expand without constriction and this reduced the pressure in her brain. They took out a piece about 15 cm x 8 cm. Two emergency life-saving operations in two days. The gods were smiling on us as Spain's premier neurosurgeon

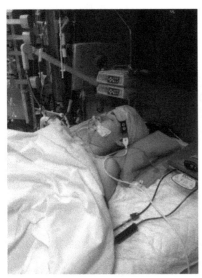

was based in San Sebastian. By now we were exhausted and struggling to cope. We sat by Evie's bed, staring at our amazing daughter, wondering what she had done to deserve this.

We realised almost immediately that trying to stay in control and cope with all of the medical information was going to be impossible if we did it alone, so I rang Tim and Mary, friends of ours who lived near Carcassonne, a four-and-a-half-hour drive away in France. Like the true friends they are, they dropped everything and drove to be with us in San Sebastian and stayed until we left. They shared our apartment, cooked, cleaned, and did the washing; things that we didn't have the capacity to do. This gave us the energy to concentrate on Evie exclusively, and without them, things would have been much tougher. Our days developed into a routine quickly. We were up at six, in the car to the hospital by six-thirty, and we stayed there until they threw us out at nine that evening. Back to the apartment to eat the lovely dinner that Mary had prepared, bed, and then we'd do it all again the next day.

Evie was now in a stable induced coma and, at this point, the accepted opinion was that the tumour was most probably benign and slow-growing as there had been so few symptoms beforehand. We were blissfully ignorant of what was to come. We were discussing major surgery to remove the rest of the tumour within the next 10–14 days, and planning for 8–12 months of chemo and radio therapy. Getting her home would come after the surgery. We were expecting her to have a year off school before returning to re-start year eight. Tough on Evie and on all of us, but doable. I instinctively knew that we could get her through it because we loved her so much.

Finally, after extensive discussions between San Sebastian and the Bristol Royal Children's Hospital, the decision was taken to fly her home where the remaining surgery could be carried out using Bristol's interoperative MRI scanner to guide the removal of the tumour. After eight days in intensive care in Spain, Evie was flown home by air ambulance to Bristol on Wednesday 31 October. Thank God for the EHIC card and decent insurance; the total bill for nine days in the ICU, two emergency operations, and an ICU flight home in a private jet with an ICU nurse and doctor came to nearly €500,000!

The following afternoon I arrived in Bristol, having driven up through France. We met the oncology team and were told that not only was the tumour malignant, but it was highly aggressive and treatment wouldn't be effective. She had a grade IV diffuse midline glioma. Evie was dying, it was just a case of how long. Initial estimates at that stage gave us six or maybe nine months if we were lucky. After two more operations, eight days in the PICU, and three weeks in the High Dependency Unit, we brought Evie home to be near her friends and family. Another MRI on 24 November had revealed that the tumour was growing rapidly. She had a life expectancy of two weeks, but through sheer guts and determination she survived for six. The surgery in Spain had damaged her short-term memory, so thankfully she knew little about her prognosis. The hardest thing I have ever had to do in my life was tell my beautiful 13-year-old daughter that she had cancer. Her only response was "People die from that don't they?" and ten minutes later she had forgotten the conversation ever happened.

At home we needed the combined help of nurses from CLIC Sargent and Julia's House Hospice, our GP and the oncology team at the Royal United Hospital Bath to manage her condition and medication. We turned the dining room into a bedroom for her. Hospital bed, hoist, wheelchair, drugs: lots of drugs. Drugs for pain, drugs for sickness and seizures, and more drugs to counter the side effects of the first batch of drugs, all of which had to be tracked and forecast ahead so that we had sufficient stocks in over Christmas and the New Year. Our once active girl was paralysed down her left-hand side, had hearing and sight loss on the left side, and was doubly incontinent. Throughout her time at home, she was visited by her friends, laughed and joked and teased both Patsy and myself in her own special way. We had a private showing of Paddington 2, which was still in the cinema, and Ward Thomas, one of her favourite bands played just for her and a friend in our lounge. I looked on as this once vibrant, intelligent girl faded away.

Throughout Evie's time at home she ate well, although it became more difficult for her in the last few days. Ken and Emma, Patsy's brother and his partner, would regularly have a box of cakes delivered from Patisserie Valerie; Evie loved them and devoured the lot. I asked her on one day what she wanted for lunch and she said, "Scallops please, Daddy!" so off I went into Devizes to find some for her. We gave her whatever she wanted, whenever she wanted it. We ate once she was asleep, which was usually after 8 pm. In the three months that Evie was ill, I didn't prepare Patsy and myself a single meal. Sam, our wonderful neighbour, organised the rest of our neighbours to provide us with meals on a continual basis. All we had to do was reheat it. It gave us the chance to give Evie 100% of our attention. Keep in mind that she did this for over three months. Truly wonderful, and we are indebted to her, and Andy, as well as all of our wonderful neighbours. Not surprisingly, as Evie's tumour grew larger she ate less and less, and towards the end she mostly ate yoghurt and fruit.

Bringing Evie home from hospital for those last few precious weeks was undoubtedly the right thing to do. Had she stayed on the ward, I am convinced that she would have died sooner and wouldn't have been anywhere near as happy. At home she had her cats with her, could see her friends far more easily, and we were away from the rigid structure of a hospital routine. No waking her up at two o'clock in the morning for her obs. We could be with her all day, every day, and that was worth its weight in gold. Evie's comfort and needs were paramount.

Most children that get a brain tumour have it for many months or years, and undergo extensive treatment along the way. Evie's was so rare, so aggressive, that it all seemed to be over in the blink of an eye. After her autopsy we found out that, at the end, her tumour was doubling in size every six days. In amongst the pain, we managed to talk about tissue donation. We couldn't donate her organs, because she died from cancer, but we were able to donate the tumour and affected brain tissue to a live brain tumour trial that was taking place in Nottingham. It didn't give us any peace as such, but at least she may just help find a better treatment for someone else.

At just after noon on 11th January 2018 Evie died. The pressure of the tumour on her hippocampus was too much. Our world collapsed. The girl that we loved so much was gone forever.

Chapter 2

The Unknown

Being a bereaved parent is like nothing else you've ever known. Your whole purpose in life is gone. Agony, disbelief, constant questioning. Just when you need your friends the most, they disappear like a wisp. Compared to some, we have been extremely lucky as we have escaped the aggression that others have experienced, or the blinding ignorance from family members that blights their future. We have a hard core of close, loyal friends that have stood by us. They have been there when we needed them, and remain with us to this day. But so many others have melted away, either unsure what to say, or petrified that losing a child might be contagious. Ironically, just when you are at your lowest ebb, and need the comfort of friends, they abandon you. My faith in the majority of humanity has now dissolved. People tell me that others avoid us because they fear upsetting us by saying the wrong thing. Do they give any consideration to the fact that staying away hurts even more? The message that it sends to us is, "I don't care enough about your child to make the effort." As we were to discover quite quickly, losing your child isolates you socially, and the loneliness is unbelievable. Yes, we have each other, but that isn't enough. Nowhere near enough.

Even when Evie was ill people avoided us. I had to lie to her when she asked why two of her 'supposed' best friends hadn't been to see her; one never even bothered to send a 'get well' card. I told Evie that they were really busy at school and probably couldn't get the time away. I lied to save her the pain of knowing that they just didn't care. I was ashamed of myself for doing it, and furious at the mothers who had taught their daughters that when your friend is dying, it's okay to abandon them. 'Abandon' may seem like a harsh word in this context, but that is exactly what it felt like. None of the best rational explanations or reasoning in this world is going to convince me otherwise. This was one of those early times when I began to figure out that I had changed at my core. Everything that we once knew or accepted as normal had changed. Logic didn't hold water any more. Emotions are erratic, volatile, and unpredictable. Perception is now more important than fact or intention. I can be 'fine' one minute, raging the next, and plumbing the depths of despair shortly after that. It has also taught me something else, sadly: hate. There are some people out there that I will never forgive. I'm not proud of it, but Evie is gone and I can't change what people did to her.

It wasn't all bad by any means. A few close friends were incredible. Evie's very best friend Izzy was struggling, but her answer when questioned if she was happy to see Evie was, "What sort of friend would I be if I didn't? Compared to what she is going through, my pain is nothing." When she was with Evie she laughed and

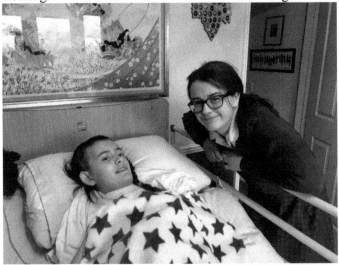

smiled. When she was out of sight she cried. When Izzy

was here, Evie smiled, laughed, and we relaxed a little. Seeing two close friends just being together was lovely. Evie so looked forward to seeing Izzy whenever we told her she was coming over. It introduced some kind of normality into her life. Having Mummy and Daddy around is one thing, but you can't beat seeing your friends. At Evie's funeral, in her eulogy I said that Evie had taught us the meaning of true friendship, and that holds true to this day.

When Evie was in the High Dependency Unit, Patsy and I developed a routine. I would leave our charity accommodation at Ronald McDonald House and go down first at about half six to give Evie her breakfast – she still ate incredibly well – then Patsy would join us a little later to relieve me. During that first hour each day Evie was often still asleep, so I would potter around on the internet, and then one day a phrase popped into my head and I decided to write it down; I wrote a poem. I have no idea why I decided to do it, especially as I hate poetry of any kind. I can't get to grips with it. I find all of it hard to read and my brain doesn't work that way. So, I wrote it down in one go, and then promptly forgot about it. After Evie died, I went back to that poem and added two more verses. On and off over the next few months I wrote a few more poems, but only when a phrase popped into my head. They aren't in here because they are exceptionally bad. I'm not being modest – trust me – they are dreadful.

After Evie died, we still received regular visits from both CLIC Sargent and Julia's House Hospice, all part of their post-loss care package. We talked about a whole load of things that were affecting us, and they offered possible coping strategies. One of the ideas that was suggested to Patsy was writing her feelings down, keeping a journal. The concept was that you find the act of writing cathartic, and then over time you can look back and see the changes that have taken place, to prove to yourself that you aren't static. The idea didn't appeal to Patsy, so we moved on.

I've never been one for diaries and the like, so pretty much ignored the idea of writing until many months later.

As I said earlier, the world of a bereaved parent is like nothing else you've ever encountered. Nothing can prepare you for what happens. We knew that Evie was going to die from the beginning of November until her death in January, yet that in no way helped us prepare for what was going to happen to us. We had been entirely focused on Evie, her health and wellbeing, and keeping her as pain-free as possible. The impact of losing a child attacks every part of your being. Exhaustion, permanent exhaustion, was not something I was expecting. I wake up every morning feeling like I have been awake all night, and that someone has taken my eyes out and rolled them in sand. This happens every day no matter how well I sleep. You become totally lethargic and lose motivation for anything. And I mean anything. For some, just getting up in the morning is more than they can manage. As you will hear many times, grief affects people in different ways, and understanding that is vital if you are to survive. Firstly, because you can't necessarily look to others for a hint about what is coming next, and secondly because your partner, if you have one, will be experiencing something totally different. There's little common ground, and that can be incredibly difficult to deal with.

Because you are emotionally vulnerable, you can't predict how you will react to certain things. I came across all sorts of triggers that I wasn't expecting. I was kind of expecting certain things like her birthday or the anniversary of her death to be hard. But it was the unexpected ones that caught me out. When 'Strictly Come Dancing' started in 2018 I was a wreck. Evie loved it, and when she was little she would stand on my toes and we would dance around the lounge to each routine. When Evie was three, she and I 'won' the whole competition! Well, Mummy was the only judge, so it wasn't a huge surprise! When new films that she would have liked were released, like Despicable Me 3, I fell just a little bit further. Watching her friends grow and choose their GCSEs, things that Evie would never do, was painful. The emotional battering that I took in that first year was unbelievable. I felt as if I needed to wear body armour just to go out, to keep the world at bay.

Then I started to think about the 'that'll never happen' stuff. She'll never graduate from university, I'll never teach her to drive, she'll never have a boyfriend, she'll never get married, I'll never be a grandfather. I'll never hand over those hundreds of bottles of 2004 wine to her to enjoy as she got older. We've not only lost our girl: we've lost a great chunk of our future too.

One of the toughest things to face is the isolation. You can become socially isolated very quickly unless you are ready for it. Make no mistake, part of the reason for this is the lack of motivation I have mentioned above; I found I couldn't be bothered to go out. It was too much effort; far easier to stay in and watch TV. It can become a self-fulfilling prophecy very quickly. Even though I had no energy, and even less enthusiasm for anything, I forced myself and Patsy to go out, to see friends, to do stuff, because if we didn't do it we would have become house-bound. There were, and still are, days when it is all too hard and I sit and watch a Bond film for a couple of hours to let the world pass me by. I used to feel guilty about it, but not anymore. If you don't look after yourself, then you won't be fit to look after your wife/husband/surviving kids.

I guess the main point that I am trying to make here is that it took me at least a year to figure out that the rules of the game had changed, and what I was going through was totally new to me. I had to accept that I was going to have to learn quickly, adapt, and roll with it. The alternative was something that I couldn't even think about. I have always been an optimist, a real glass-half-full person. But that resolve was tested beyond breaking point time and again. It took a vast amount of determination to keep coming back from the brink and for me two things kept me going:

the love that I have for Patsy, and the certain knowledge that if I met Evie again too soon, she would be furious that her life had been snatched from her, yet here was I prepared to throw mine away. It somehow seemed disloyal. The depression that her death caused can be so deep and so dark some days that life really isn't worth living.

At some point in the spring of 2019, I made an unconscious decision to accept that I couldn't bring Evie back, at least for a while, and fight back against the pain. Fight to carry on. I can't say when it happened, but it meant that I had a focus again, not quite something to live for, but enough to just keep going for a while. But I couldn't carry on alone, I needed external help in whatever form it might come. As an ex-RAF pilot, I had been trained to find solutions to problems under any circumstances. I had always seen problems as a solution that I hadn't found yet. But this was different in so many ways. For the first time in my life, I couldn't find the solution on my own, I was going to need help from a whole range of different sources. Asking for help was a huge step for me to take, not because I saw it as failure, but because I had never needed to do it before, and didn't know how.

One of the very first things that we did in the spring of 2018 was join The Compassionate Friends. We joined our local support group within a few weeks of Evie's death, went on a weekend retreat in the Dales and also joined the closed Facebook group, including the Childless Parents group. And this is where the point of this book started. In early 2019, one of the mums in the group suggested posting pictures of things that gave them strength, which for her was her surviving children. The idea was picked up by a couple of other parents. The moderators asked these parents to be mindful of the parents who didn't have any other children, who might find the posts upsetting. Long story short, the idea was dropped, but the suggestion around things giving us strength gave me an idea. On

Twitter there is a regular thing called #wednesdaywisdom, usually a whole load of mindless clichés: stuff that people have found on the internet. I suggested that maybe we could do our own version, writing down things that we have found helpful, hints and tips, or perhaps what may have lifted us. So, the TCF Wednesday Wisdom was born. I wrote the first one, a very short piece on being kind to yourself. My posts grew in length, and expanded in their subjects to include what I found difficult as well, and then a few people started to suggest that I publish them so that other bereaved parents might gain something.

I have always written the Wednesday Wisdoms in one go, then just cut and paste the piece for that week into Facebook when I needed to. I'm usually a couple of weeks ahead of myself, if that makes sense. I don't want it to be written to a deadline and fake. I wrote them when some form of idea or inspiration struck. They were never forced, and I usually wrote them quickly while the idea was fresh, and only corrected the spelling and grammar before uploading them. As the weeks went on, I found writing more helpful. The idea helped me understand more clearly what was happening in my own head. As I typed, I was exploring what I had written in my mind, expanding on the thought process as I went. I then started posting them on the Evie's Gift Facebook page too, so that friends and family could better understand what we are going through. To so many of us, the 'muggles' out there have absolutely no concept of the level of pain that we are in 24 hours a day. I hoped that the posts might be helpful for the wider community. But, mainly, I was doing it for me, to unload my pain. It was purely selfish.

One day, after some nudges on FB from friends, I decided to start writing this book, a short introduction at the front, followed by a collection of the Wednesday Wisdom posts. But it has developed from there and now, although the posts were my original purpose, I've decided to write about losing your child in a wider sense as well, mostly from a father's perspective, although it isn't a commentary on a man's view. The posts follow, but for now, the next sections focus on life as a bereaved parent, and on how it unfolded for me, for us. The pain, the utter emptiness that we feel all day, every day, and the rank stupidity of so many people that we know. If you hadn't guessed, I'm currently in the 'angry' phase. That anger has undoubtedly coloured the tone of this book, but it is also a true reflection of how I feel, so I'm not going to tone it down. This book is for me as much as anyone else, so if I am to gain from the experience then it has to be a true and accurate reflection of what I am feeling. To do otherwise would defeat the healing that it helps to bring.

If you are looking for solutions to your newly-bereaved world, then I'm afraid you might be disappointed. But maybe, by seeing that someone else's life is falling apart, that a once strong, focused, and determined air force pilot can be reduced to a broken wreck, then you'll realise that you aren't alone, that there are others out there feeling the same as you and that a metaphorical reassuring hand on your arm is just an email or text away.

Chapter 3

The Compassionate Friends

We joined The Compassionate Friends very shortly after Evie's funeral. We also joined our local support group and went to our first meeting. For the first time, we were amongst people who understood everything that we were experiencing. It was a revelation. Likeminded individuals who didn't judge us which was, and still is, incredibly liberating. The first meeting was incredibly difficult, and I came away saying that I had never experienced such a room full of pain. At that stage I wasn't sure that I would keep going, and it wasn't helped by the fact that I was the only bloke there. We took pictures of Evie with us and gradually we started to look forward to the monthly meetings, as they were the only time that we could drop the mask for a couple of hours and be our true selves, the pain open and evident for all to see in its raw state. To be able to reveal your vulnerability to others, while feeling safe, is incredibly helpful. A year later, we have become friends, knowing that any of us could ring another at 3 am and need to talk, and that we'd be listened to. That's a rare quality in any group, and one that we treasure.

The Compassionate Friends as a charity is unusual in that everyone there, the staff, trustees, and volunteers are all bereaved parents – in effect they are all 'service-users'. Most charities have little experience of their cause at each and every level. This brings one major benefit to the organisation – they speak from personal knowledge and experience, and that is invaluable. They've all been through what you and I are facing and have survived. They don't hide their pain but they do give you the time and space to do and say what you need to. By looking at them you can see that you can survive this, that somewhere, sometime, a light will appear at the end of the tunnel. Like all bereaved parents, their stories are different and they have different experiences and needs, but they share a common goal of wanting to help others.

Just two months into our bereavement journey we went to a TCF weekend retreat in Derbyshire for newly-bereaved parents. We walked through the door to be greeted by a heart-warming hug from Carolyn, the CEO. It wasn't forced or fake, it was a genuine welcome from a total stranger who knew what we were feeling. That set the tone for the next two days. We picked our talks and everyone ate together. The masks stayed down for two days and we listened and learned, as much about ourselves as others. We also spent a lot of time making a tealight holder out of an old jam jar. I was cynical. I didn't feel like being 10 all over again, but you know what? Not only was it good fun, but we chatted away to other parents about Evie, and listened to their stories about their children too. We laughed and remembered. It was a relaxing way to spend time doing something that we could keep. In fact, we light a candle to Evie every night now, and use it an awful lot.

The lovely thing about the retreats is that you can throw yourself into it, or just sit and listen, there's no pressure either way. It's just reassuring to be around people in the same horrible position as you and feel no embarrassment when you can't keep it together. It isn't all a bed of roses though. We went to a Childless Parents Retreat a few months after the first one and we struggled enormously. We came away battered emotionally from so many difficult stories, but from it we figured out that there's always someone in a worse place than you, no matter what your story. It didn't scare us off though, as we booked for the same event again. I took a lot of gin just in case.

One of the reassuring things about TCF is that they are always there with advice or information, and because they've all been through it you won't get fobbed off with platitudes. Our support group is now evolving into a friends' group and the dynamic is shifting slowly. We know each other well enough to be brutally honest and I am sure that it will develop further. But even if it doesn't, what we have now is such an enormous help. It is a wonderful charity and if you haven't joined, I strongly recommend that you do.

The ability to meet others at retreats who were further along than we were helped us figure out what the hell was happening. It helped us to tackle the complete feeling of emptiness and loss. Now though, we sit with others who are newly-bereaved themselves and can offer those same words of reassurance that we were given on our first retreat. In some small way, being able to give something to a complete stranger helps us heal too, and that is the magic of this lovely little charity.

Chapter 4

Friends and Family

We've been lucky compared to some when it comes to our family. All of them have been supportive, and at just over 18 months after Evie's death, they are still there when we need them. We recently spent a long weekend with Ken and Emma, my brother-in-law and his partner, and for the first time in a long while we were able to just be ourselves, be what we needed to be. We could participate, we could crawl away and hide, or just be quiet and thoughtful. They are such natural, understanding people that there was no pressure to do or say anything, we could just 'be'. There are moments sometimes when you are chatting about something trivial when a memory strikes that sends you down into the depths. It may not last long, but it takes you out of the conversation for a while. Ken and Emma are such beautiful people that being around them gives us strength and comfort all in one go. We were seeing Tim and Mary, the couple that had looked after us in San Sebastian, when one of those 'quiet' moments hit me at breakfast. I locked down emotionally, shut up completely and stared out of the window, completely lost for what to do. I got a swift kick under the table from Patsy, but I simply couldn't break out of it. Moments like that, when they come without warning, can take ages to recover from and its why so many of us simply avoid seeing others, especially in the early months. It takes a special kind of friend to sit and wait for you to come back.

Our experience of 'friends' has been mixed to say the least. At one end of the spectrum we have a small clutch of exceptional friends who understand (as much as they ever can), and give us the space and freedom to be whatever we need to be. At the opposite end are the ones that abandoned us when we needed them most. Some ran for the hills the second they found out Evie was ill, and to be frank we're better off without them. One just wanted the gossip so that she could talk about how she had 'been to see those sad people'. Our address book has changed beyond all recognition. I've seen people cross the road deliberately to avoid me, and cross back again behind me. In a supermarket, the mum of one of Evie's school friends got within six feet of me, looked up, gave a sharp intake of breath (which could have been heard two counties away) and she turned a 90 left and strode off, head down. Coward. People tell me that these things happen because they don't know what to say. Bollocks! You don't need to 'say' anything. You give me a hug and ask how I'm coping, and when I answer, you listen, even if it is hard to hear. That's it, nothing more complicated than that, just show you actually care. Give up two minutes of your life to offer someone a little support, then carry on with your shopping. Sadly, people don't realise that their actions can have such a painful impact on a bereaved parent. One mother posted on Facebook that she couldn't come and visit because 'she had to protect her family'! From what? The last time I checked we didn't have a contagious disease, and neither of us has been accused of being an axe murderer. Evie was 13 when she died. She had spent much of her short life helping her friends, including the daughter of this mother, and yet she felt that acknowledging Evie's existence was too 'dangerous', 'difficult'? That kind of attitude is the cruellest blow. It takes a lot of energy to work past that kind of rejection.

Losing Evie pushed us to the lowest point of our lives, and we desperately needed the love and support of our friends. And at this point, when we needed them to just listen to us, most of them melted away. The hardest thing for us to accept is that by doing so, these 'friends' have demonstrated that Evie didn't matter to them, that they just want to move on with their lives and forget that she ever existed; just in case it might be contagious. But you know what, I'm not prepared to let them off the hook that lightly. I will take every opportunity to put Evie's name, her image, and her memory out there for all to see. If they want to have a go at me, fine I'll deal with it. Have a go at my wife and I'll take that too. But they have a go at my daughter, or ignore her, and I will never forgive them, because she was better than that, and would never, ever abandon a friend. More to the point, she was better than them.

Along with the bad comes the good, the wonderful friends who just keep giving, the ones who don't change the subject when you just want to talk about Evie, the ones who appear uninvited and take you out for a coffee, the ones who write sensitive comments in cards or notes for you, and never spout platitudes. They have their own lives to live, but they always remember that you are there and need a friend, and will always answer your call or text. Sometimes, this kind of help comes from where you would least expect it. It is a cliché, but also a truism, to say that a tragedy like losing a child really does show you who your real friends are. Dealing with Patsy and I can't have been easy for our friends for a myriad of reasons, but they kept doing it, again and again. I am extremely grateful to them.

There are many other people that are around for us and would help if we needed it. They feel awkward around us, unsure what to say or do, but are there anyway. They don't change the subject when we talk about Evie, but nor do they start a conversation about her either. It's a funny kind of no-mans-land, but at least with them we know that we won't be ignored. We can talk about Evie and they will listen. We can remember her and smile.

Chapter 5

Drugs and Alcohol

A slightly tongue in cheek title, but true enough. Finding ways to cope with such a massive trauma is so hard. We are all different, and until we try things out, we don't know what will work. And just to make it even more complicated, if it works today, it might not work tomorrow. The problem is that we don't have the drive, energy, or motivation to try things out. Depression comes quickly and hits hard. For me I felt like I was sliding down a steep slope of scree, hands and feet dug into the dirt trying to stop myself but failing miserably. The deeper I got, the steeper the slope became and the harder it was to find a way of stopping the slide. I started counselling within a month or so of Evie dying. It was probably too soon, but I stayed with it. It was at one of these meetings that my counsellor sensed I needed time off and we talked about what was happening at home and at work. Walking back up the hill to my car I rang the office and took the rest of the week off, just to give my head time to calm down.

For months after her death, my head was racing, desperately trying to find the solution to the problem that was Evie's death. I am task-driven, and my brain was treating her death just like any other problem to be solved. Break it down into its component parts, solve each one, re-build, and 'bingo', Evie is back. To me it was that simple. But it was soaking up massive amounts of energy and brain capacity. It was exhausting because it never stopped, the white noise in my head never went away. Finally, after another couple of months I went to the doctor and walked out with a prescription for anti-depressants. The noise started to abate and I started to get some capacity back; not a lot, but enough to start functioning again. I regained the ability to think and rationalise things. They didn't take away the pain, but the lows were now shallower and less frequent. The pills don't work for everyone, and some will actively avoid them. Is there still a stigma to taking them? Absolutely, but I don't care. They help me and that is good enough. After more than a year taking the pills, the dosage has increased, and if I miss one, I know it within a few hours. Not long ago I felt as if I was ready to start easing back away from them, but a bad period put paid to that idea. The point here is that it doesn't matter. You take whatever time you need. I've noticed that just like Evie's death itself, people find talking about depression and anti-depressants a tough subject to deal with. Why should that be? I'm the one taking the pills, not them. I can't do Evie's life justice or be there for Patsy if I'm a wreck, so taking anti-depressants makes sense. In the early days, some of the side effects were a little unpleasant, but now they've either subsided or I've got used to living with them. The most noticeable side effect is that they make me hot: my body temperature has increased somehow, or at least it feels that way.

A glass of wine or two also helps. We talked about it the other day and we don't actually drink any more now than we did before Evie fell ill, but it allows you to hide for a little while and let your mind and soul recover. A drink gives you an excuse to drift, to forget the pain for a bit. It washes the stress away for a while. It is so tempting to open a bottle of wine every night, but we've not done that. I'm not sure how we have managed to avoid it, but we have. I can understand how easy it is to slip into a routine of drinking, which then becomes drinking heavily.

Wine was always a passion of mine, and for the first year or so after Evie's death it simply became an alcoholic liquid in a glass. The pleasure was gone. I had lost the pleasure in understanding the wine, its structure, balance, and how it complemented the meal. I still don't have the passion for it that I used to, but I'm allowing myself to enjoy it more, and have started to think about matching food and wine more carefully again. I still feel guilty when I enjoy the wine, not because it's wine, but because Evie will never experience it or know how lovely food and wine combinations can be. I feel guilty about enjoying anything when she's not here, but that's a wider problem.

I don't get drunk, or abuse alcohol, but I do enjoy a drink when I feel the need. A bad day at the office, approaching a milestone such as Evie's birthday or the anniversary of her death, all make me head for the cork-screw. The wine doesn't interfere with the pills; strangely, grapefruit does, which I can't quite work out. Good job they don't make wine out of grapefruit.

Chapter 6

Words and Language

I always told Evie "It's not what you say, but how you say it." We are incredibly vulnerable and the wrong word or phrase can trigger a major reaction. People, friends, and colleagues want to help. They say things in the hope that they will lift us because they want to make us 'better' or cheer us up. What they singularly fail to realise is that we will never be better. Whoever wrote the phrase, 'Time is a great healer', clearly never lost a child. They have created a great pile of platitudinous crap. Time …. is a daily reminder that your child still isn't there with you. You don't heal: you just get more experienced at carrying the pain and better at hiding it.

When people ask "How are you?" they hope for and expect you to say, "Fine," because they can't cope with the honest truth; it is too much for them to deal with. They can wander off to their little worlds, happy in the knowledge that they have done their bit and talked to the bereaved parent. Tick. Job done, filed. What they don't realise is that you need someone to listen to you when you answer, "Actually, the last few weeks have been pretty rubbish. Mother's Day without her was empty, I felt alone. Work expect me to be back to normal and have 'moved on', and all I want to do sometimes is stay in bed and cry." What a bereaved parent needs is someone to ask how they are and then listen to a truthful answer. Be prepared to give us a hug if we start to wobble, or just put a hand on our arm when it is needed. And keep on doing it.

Unlike the loss of a parent, and we've lost three out of four, the loss of a child is something that you don't 'move on' from. It's all in the wrong order. My dad was 78 when he died, Patsy's mum and dad were 86 and 84. I'm sure the psychiatrists have a very long and complex explanation for why this is, but for me it is simpler. Patsy and I created Evie out of nothing but love, in effect we 'made' her. When she died, part of us died with her. As she was our only child, Evie's death made us childless parents. We're back to being a couple again, no other children, and too old to try for more. We can't move on because our world has shifted fundamentally. It's almost like living in a parallel universe. We will grow old without her. We will die without her to leave everything to. What do we do with all the family heirlooms that we have collected? Who will be their custodian now?

Words and language are so important when you are low or vulnerable. Certain phrases can be intensely annoying, and at times it is almost as if you are hypersensitive to what people say and how they say it. In many cases, that sensitivity isn't rational or sensible. People begin sentences with "It's not the same as losing a child, but when my dog died … ". If it's not the same then shut up and don't say it. They offer meaningless platitudes like, "Evie wouldn't want you to be sad." Really? How do you know? Maybe she's intensely angry that she's dead and blames us for something? In all probability, if I could have a meaningful conversation with her, she would hopefully express something positive about how Patsy and I carry on our lives without her. But she was 13 when she died, and I'm pretty certain that, given the choice, she wouldn't want to be dead either.

For parents who have surviving children, the phrase, "Well at least you have other children", can send them into a tailspin, because it belittles the child that they have lost and somehow devalues them. Again, it isn't deliberate, but because the world of a bereaved parent is so alien to everyone else, they are at a loss for what to say. So, instead of asking something caring and sensible like "How are her brothers coping?", they spout some trite nonsense.

The words that we, and others, use are very particular for us. For me, saying that Evie has 'passed away' is unfair on her and seems to make light of it. She died. From cancer. She certainly didn't pass away from the Big C. Say it the way it is. Who do we use these phrases for? For us or those around us who struggle to cope with the language? What you choose to say is entirely up to you, of course, but I prefer to say it the way it is. Death isn't pleasant so let's not cover it up. But just as importantly, how we interpret what is said can prejudice our world and how we see others.

So, thinking about what people say to us, what do we 'hear' when they speak? Here are a few examples from Google Translate for Bereaved Parents:

- How are You?
  - Please say 'fine', please say 'fine', please say 'fine'. I can't cope with anything else. The last thing I need is you to start crying, I've got the kids to collect from school.
- You're so brave.
  - Errr, I'm struggling to think of anything helpful to say, so I'll say something that might be taken as a compliment.
- You're an inspiration.
  - Hey, I'm doing really well here, that's two compliments I can tick off.
- Have you had a lovely birthday/ anniversary/Christmas?
  - I'd forgotten completely that your child is dead.

The perception of what is said outweighs the words themselves, and our mood at the time is crucial. Sometimes the questions just get lost in the noise, other times they are intensely annoying.

At a recent TCF support group meeting we got talking about language and the things that people say to us. This led into 'Platitude Bingo'. Those delightful little phrases that people say that can appear so heartless or just utterly puerile. I find them intensely irritating and that level of irritation hasn't diminished over time. I have added in the response that I often feel like giving. So, how many of these have you heard?

- God needed another angel. *Really? Then why not pick someone else?*
- She's in a better place. *No! She isn't! The best place for her is here with me.*
- Time is a great healer. *Rubbish! Time will never heal this.*
- You're still young/you have the rest of your life ahead of you. *I don't want it!*
- She wouldn't want you to be sad/angry/etc. *Oh, do shut up!*
- You're so strong/amazing/inspirational. *No, I'm not. I'm surviving because I have no choice.*
- I don't know how you manage. *Christ, neither do I!*
- At least you still have her brother/sister/dog/gerbil. *If you don't leave soon, I'm going to hit you.*

And my personal favourite:
- Everything happens for a reason. *Don't be a prat. Pick a window, you're leaving.*

So, what could you ask or say? How can you talk to a bereaved parent in a way that is kind, thoughtful and caring? Everyone is different, and will respond in different ways, so providing a list of phrases doesn't really work. But you can do a few things that will help enormously. Firstly, stop and think about what you are going to say. Is it sincere or are you just trying to find something to say to fill the time? Avoid platitudes and meaningless statements. But most importantly, listen and listen well. Put aside any discomfort that you may feel and give the bereaved parent your undivided attention for a little while; after all you will feel uncomfortable for a few minutes, they will feel dreadful for the rest of their life. Ask how they really are, tell the parent that you miss their child. Hearing another person say your child's name is a wonderful gift because it shows that they haven't been forgotten.

Chapter 7

Men are from Mars, Women are from Venus,
or Mars, or Southend,
or Somewhere Completely Different

The first thing that anyone tells you about mourning is that we all deal with our grief in different ways. That is an absolute truth. Patsy and I have dealt with it in entirely different ways, almost polar opposites. We have not really understood what is happening to the other and therefore struggle to help. We all have different needs and different pains. We have been different all of our lives and so why wouldn't we be different in grief too? If you believe in the signs of the zodiac stuff, Patsy is an Aries and I am a Cancer; a fire sign and a water sign, complete opposites. It's what keeps things interesting when life is going well. Losing a child places incredible stress in any relationship. There is data that suggests that the divorce rate amongst bereaved parents is 83%; that's more than four in five marriages that fail. More pain. Men and women struggle to understand each other properly when things are fine, so when this amount of stress and trauma is thrown into the mix, is it any wonder that things fall apart? Obviously, I was very aware of Patsy's pain so I tried to help, and walked on those eggshells for a long time before I realised I was being ridiculous. That's not entirely honest – my counsellor told me very clearly to 'back off'. So, I stopped and just acted as normally as I could, but still wanted to be there as a safety net when she needed me. I still avoid certain phrases or things that I know will annoy her, but I'm not frightened of a bad reaction any more. I give her the space to deal with it. I've accepted that no matter how much I might want to, I can't take the pain away.

Men have a reputation for taking their feelings, sticking them in a box, and burying them. The stereotype is that women are more open about their feelings. Bollocks. I've seen women hide from the pain and men in floods of tears pouring out their anguish, completely broken. The fact is we are all different so we have to be aware of that. You can't make assumptions about gender, or anything else for that matter. The differences between people become ever more obvious after losing a child, and the gender of the person isn't the issue: it's the fact that we have to be aware of just how different we are. We have to learn to listen in a whole new way. Understand that, just because something works for me, doesn't mean that it will work for my wife. It might even have the opposite effect. I started taking anti-depressants about four months after Evie died, Patsy has never taken them. Early on, I tried to push Patsy towards them because I had experienced a positive effect, but that was the wrong thing to do. She dug her heels in and that was that. I shouldn't have been surprised because that's exactly what she has done for the last 31 years of marriage.

The path of grief isn't clear, doesn't go in a straight line, and the pace at which you move along it is completely different for everyone. There are no assumptions that you can make: everything that you once knew about your partner no longer applies. The shock to your system is so staggeringly huge that it will take a lifetime to understand it. So, don't try. Be patient, listen, and give them space. Be there as a safety net if things go badly wrong. But above all, learn, and learn quickly. It would be great to be able to say, 'here is a list of things to do that will help'. But that list doesn't exist. There's no silver bullet or magic cure. A list for me may not work for you. You must discover it for yourself. Be prepared to get it wrong and learn from your mistakes. And learn to apologise straight away. These things don't come naturally to people, but you must change if you want to avoid blistering rows that end in tears. After all, you created a life together, so presumably you love your partner still?

There's a lovely graph that someone drew which shows the five stages of grief, as if it is all so predictable and easy to follow – denial, anger, bargaining, depression, and acceptance. What about all of those other feelings that don't sit nicely into one of those five nice neat phases? After eight weeks you'll be here, after six months you'll be here. Not a chance, you bounce around all over the place. Back and forth, speed up, slow down, and then come crashing down again for no reason at all. Then some complete moron at work makes some crass remark that knocks you back months. So, while I am currently most definitely in an angry phase, Patsy is feeling lost again. I have no idea if the angry phase will end quickly, or whether I will come back to it again in a year, or five years. Or maybe it will suddenly end, and I'll find myself in 'acceptance' – whatever that is. I do know that before Evie died, I didn't suffer fools gladly. Now I don't suffer them at all, period. When I see a post on Facebook that someone has had a bad day at work and is angry, I think, 'get over it, nobody died'. That's where my marker is now – has someone died? Everything else is a frustration, nothing more. My everyday life has distilled into something that is black or white, with little or no grey. At one extreme is death, at the other is everything else. It's that simple, anything other than death is unimportant. Brexit? Who cares? Donald Trump or Boris Johnson spout some trite nonsense. So what? Scratched car? Oh well. A lady drove into the back of my car and it was written off. I shrugged my shoulders.

One of the differences between Patsy and myself is that I have felt Evie nearby a few times. Patsy hasn't. I can't explain how or why, but on a number of occasions, I knew she was there with me. A few days after she died, I swear I saw her looking in at us when we were out with Ken and Emma, having a cup of tea. Once, very early on, I had been to her grave and reached the point where I needed to leave. As I walked away, I sensed or heard, "Daddy don't go!" So I turned around and went back. We were at a Ward Thomas concert in Marlborough and I am certain I felt her head lean against my arm, as she would have been sat between Patsy and I. Was I imagining it? Was it just hope? Probably. So what? That feeling brought peace for just a moment and that is worth more than anything else. Patsy hasn't felt anything like that, and hasn't dreamt of her very much either. I have had just a few dreams about Evie, and each time she hasn't said anything, just looked at me. In the last one, which was some time ago, she was in my arms laughing. I've been toying with the idea of visiting a medium, but I don't know if I'm ready. If it is a failure, I'll feel terrible and angry. If it is 'successful' I'll be sceptical, so it seems to me that it is almost a lose-lose situation. What we both think and feel is quite different, and we are both right because by definition we can't be wrong. You draw strength where you can.

Finding coping strategies is incredibly important for my sanity. Patsy has struggled to find something that gives her peace, even for a while. Walking has turned out to bring some tranquillity and I have found it be the only time when my mind is quiet. The noise stops and I can almost talk to Evie in a way that I feel at peace with. I don't mean a stroll to the shops – I mean many miles without company. Walking long distance is peaceful, calming and … well, just quiet. I can't explain why, but when I have a pack on my back and I am striding out in the countryside, my head empties of everything. I don't think about work, family, or even the loss of Evie. She wanders into my thoughts and wanders out again. I do talk out loud to her, but it isn't the same troubled thoughts that I have everywhere else. Walking isn't something that I started after Evie died. I had walked the whole South Pembrokeshire coastal path, 186 miles, in nine and a half days in May 2017, and had planned to walk 175 miles of the South West coastal path in seven days in May 2018. Evie fell ill in October 2017, and died in January the next year. I hadn't done any training and wasn't fit enough to take on 25 miles a day of coast path, so I delayed the South West walk until October 2018. Evie's godfather, David, came with me and we completed the walk. But .... I didn't get the same peace that I had experienced when walking alone. David and I have organised two 13-mile walks along the Jurassic Coast as fundraisers for Evie's Gift, and each time I have set out 15 minutes ahead of the pack to check the safety of the route on the day and warn the walkers about broken rails, bulls in fields and so on. In this way, I'm still there with everyone, but get the solitude that I'm seeking. Having done two chunky walks as fundraisers in Pembrokeshire and Cornwall, I felt that a third in quick succession wasn't reasonable, so planned my next hike to be just for me; it didn't stay like that though, as fundraising at work was getting really tough. But that's not the point. I needed to do a big walk, which was a serious test of my mental stamina.

Starting at 7:20 am on 22 June 2019, I walked for 24 hours non-stop, ostensibly to be alone, walk and think. I walked 53.4 miles, carrying everything that I needed, including water, and by the finish, near Wallingford, I was exhausted but I found the time refreshingly empty. The usual work and family pressures didn't intervene while I was walking. I was at peace with myself, with life and with everyone. I just forgot the emotional pain for a whole day and was alone with my thoughts. I didn't even really look at the countryside that much, I just put my head down and ploughed on. I probably get as much benefit from one good long walk as I do from a week away. When Patsy walks with me, I don't think that she gets that same benefit, but she enjoys the exercise – when I walk slow enough to allow her to keep up!

Patsy and I have joined a local walking club, but for me it isn't quite right. Too many voices. I end up 500 metres ahead of the rest because I want to be alone with Evie. Walking has become my quiet time. The club walkers are lovely, but I find that I want to talk to Evie, so end up away from the group. It's a bit anti-social of me, I know, but whenever I have tried walking slowly, my stride length has to change, my boots rub in different places and it's all very uncomfortable. It's more of a social thing than a walking thing I suppose.

Patsy quite likes the walking club atmosphere because most of the members don't really know about Evie, and for some reason we don't get asked the 'have you got children' question. She moves about the group chatting about this and that. A totally different approach, but it seems to work for her so that's fine. If the group were made up of parents that knew Evie, the dynamic would be so different that I don't think we would have joined. The parents of Evie's friends treat us differently now, even those that understand. They aren't doing it on purpose, but there is a look in their eyes that almost portrays fear. The fear of saying the wrong thing, or causing upset inadvertently.

About five months after Evie's death, we went to a prize giving at her old junior school, as we had created a prize in her name for the student that displayed 'Loyalty and Friendship' beyond their peer group. One of the fathers there stood in front of us and moaned for 10 minutes solid on how he was fed up with being a 'dad taxi', running around after his kids, and how he just wanted some peace. And before you think it, yes, he did know that Evie had died, as he was in our year group. I was stunned into silence; I would have given anything to be a dad taxi again, taking Evie to table tennis, or swimming, or to see a friend. And here, this fool was wittering on about how inconvenient it was that he had to give up his time for them. How I didn't just punch him in the head, I don't know. Patsy wasn't bothered by it as much as me, and just moved on. Guess I am from Mars after all, as Mars is the bringer of war, and at that moment I was ready for war.

Chapter 8

Birthdays, Anniversaries, and Milestones

The first anniversary of Evie's death was devastating. There is no other word for it. The pain came pouring back. We took the day off work and went to her grave, then went for a walk. We didn't really talk much, just went with our own thoughts. The obvious bad days you can see coming – birthdays, Christmas, Mother's Day, and the anniversary of your child's death. But there are others, the ones that you don't expect, and they can catch you out. For me, Father's Day had never been anything special. A card and that was it, we never made a fuss. But my first Father's Day without Evie was a shocker. I felt empty. It came as a total surprise. The second was far worse. The fortnight before the day got progressively worse, and on the day itself, I struggled to do anything at all. The pain was excruciating, the flashbacks knocked me sideways, I just want to cry all day. My body physically hurt. I had asked Patsy to buy a Father's Day card because I needed a reminder that I was still a father. She bought a card, and then traced Evie's writing from an older card. It was the most beautiful touch. I asked her to do it again for my birthday.

There are other days and events too that come out of the blue: the first school prize giving without her, suddenly not being involved in swimming galas or table tennis tournaments, walking around a supermarket in the spring and seeing a punnet of cherries, which she adored. In their own way, each event hurts. Each was a painful stab that our daughter wasn't here.

Our 31st wedding anniversary pretty much passed without notice. I have no idea how many of our friends' and family's birthdays we missed this year. We just aren't focused on that sort of thing any more. Our 32nd anniversary isn't far away as I write, and I imagine that we will both be at work as usual. If we miss your birthday or anniversary, then I'm sorry, it isn't intentional I promise.

Our own birthdays lost all meaning too, as did Christmas. Evie was fantastic at keeping secrets. She would be completely poker-faced when asked what Mummy had bought me for my birthday; she knew of course, but you would never realise that from her expression. And she loved hunting out presents. She got so excited about everyone else's birthday. Now they are completely flat, without meaning, just another day like any other that we have to survive. Christmas was even worse. We knew Christmas would be evil with everyone else getting all worked up, so we decided to volunteer for a Bath charity all day and served lunch to the lonely and homeless. We did our day, and then came home and ate chicken fajitas. We opened our presents to each other, such as they were, in silence, the fun gone forever.

Now, having gone through all of the 'firsts', we know what to expect, and are ready for the pain. We don't try and hide from the pain because that isn't possible. This handful of days each year are going to be horrible, but you can't avoid them so you just have to put the body armour on, smile, and get on with it. If you've lost a child then you will know that the week or so leading up to these events, or the anniversary of your child's death, can be quite traumatic. They are almost more painful than the day itself. It's a bit like an Exocet missile: you can see it coming but you can't get out of the way.

Chapter 9

Remembering your Child

We remember Evie all the time, literally every waking moment. She is present in my thoughts all day. But I also want the world to remember her, remember the kind, loving young woman that she was. I want a long-lasting legacy for her. I want others to remember her as well, as they go about their lives, to recall the fun that she brought, the fact that she was always ready to help out a friend. I have a pair of cufflinks made by Bristol Blue Glass with some of her ashes in them, so that I can have her close at least some of the time. My mum has a small pendant made by the same company.

Let's cut to the chase. One of the toughest ways of remembering your child is choosing their headstone. It's tough, because it slams home not only that they aren't here, but they aren't coming back either. Only dead people have headstones. How long you take to choose your headstone, if you do at all, is entirely your call and you cannot be wrong. Whatever works for you is fine. It is one of the most meaningful things that you will ever do. Take your time, because once it is in place, it is a world of pain and expense to change your mind. You have to get it right. For us, finding one that was fitting for a young woman was difficult. All the children's headstones were aimed at toddlers or babies, and the adult ones were too austere and cold. We needed something that reflected the blossoming young woman that she had become: a teenager who was an adult one minute and a child the next.

We didn't know what we wanted, or what was out there, but we had a concept in mind, so went looking for an artisan to create the right kind of memorial to our beautiful daughter. 'Memorial'. Even the language is old-fashioned. We researched for ages, trawling around the internet looking for something that we might like. We found two stone masons that we liked and went to visit both. We settled on one, Fergus, and he started to design the stone.

 There were many minor changes and visits to his studio to go over it again. Finding the right stone was equally important, and the Cumbrian slate that we chose is beautiful both wet and dry with a delicate green tinge. It is also hard-wearing and won't split in the cold weather. For the wording we wanted to avoid the clichés, so we chose "I hope you dance", the title of the Leann Womack song that we played at her funeral. It is a message from us to her, and her to us, and everyone else.

I have always found her grave to be a place to anchor myself to, and while she was cremated, I still feel as if she is there somehow. It is why we will never move away from the area – no retiring to Devon or Eastbourne for us! I could never leave her here alone; I need to be here to continue to look after her because she is forever 13.

The day before Evie's funeral I decided to create a charity in her name, in exactly the same way that many other parents have done. While we had been at the Bristol Royal Hospital for Children, we had noticed that so many parents were sleeping in their cars or on the floor because there just wasn't enough charity accommodation to go around. We had been extremely fortunate to be given a room at Ronald McDonald House, just a few minutes' walk from the hospital. So we set up Evie's Gift, a charity that supports the parents of children who have life threatening or life-limiting conditions and are in hospital far from home. I run a charity as my day job, so the work to set it up was easy enough. Why did I do it? I argued at the time that I had identified an unmet need, so it seemed sensible to go down that route. But it wasn't that simple. I needed to be making a difference. I needed to be able to help others. It was all part and parcel of the 'failed as a father' routine. Evie's Gift is doing fabulous work and while is it immensely hard work, I feel at least that Evie's name is out there and more people are aware of her, though when we have had applications from parents whose children have brain tumours, I have been a wreck for days afterwards. My job now is to make the charity financially sustainable in the longer term. If it failed, it would break me.

There are obviously hundreds of different ways for you to remember your child, from benches to trees, from Facebook pages to candles. I'm not going to list them here because it's almost self-evident. Suffice to say that we will all do what we think is right for our child and find something that will mark their lives in a suitable way.

Chapter 10

Work

Evie died on the eleventh of January 2018, her funeral was on the first of February, and we both went back to work full-time on the fifth of February. We did it for two reasons. We had been off for three and a half months on full pay and felt that we needed to get back to work to give some sort of 'pay back'. In addition, we wanted a focus, something else to think about to blot out the blinding pain that we were both feeling. For Patsy, work had always been a bit of a sanctuary from outside distractions and pain, and so she hoped it would give her eight hours each day to rest her tormented mind. It wasn't to be. For me, I was driven back by some force that I hadn't yet come to terms with – I just knew I had to get back to work.

For many months my productivity at work was hugely reduced, and I'm still not back to 100% by any means. I didn't know it at the time, but my mind was desperately trying to prove to itself that I could succeed at something, because, despite everything I had tried, I had failed to keep Evie alive, and that meant that I had failed as a father. Work gave me the opportunity to regain my mojo, if you like. Without a doubt, I expected far too much from myself. There was no way on this earth that I was going to be able to function at a level that would breed success. All I did was exhaust myself. Now, 17 months down the line, I recognise what I was trying to do and why. I'm still pushing hard, but I have now hit the proverbial wall and am backing off in an effort to stop myself from imploding. Some fathers drive themselves hard at work to hide from the pain. I'm not doing that, but the final outcome is the same: exhaustion, and possibly worse. I started to ask my counsellor about nervous breakdowns and what they were, and how I could recognise the symptoms. We talked a lot about it and I did some research on the net. Like all things on the web, no two sites agree, but the NHS website talked a lot about clinical depression and nervous breakdowns. It listed a number of physiological and physical symptoms that could be seen as warning signs. I was displaying about 80% of them to some degree of other, and the others weren't that far from what I was doing either. It was time to do something about it. I also looked at a site that talked about the signs that you had 'burnt out'; I showed all of them. Easing back at work was the first thing I had to do, then unloading more work for Evie's Gift onto other people followed. The next part was harder. Katie, my counsellor, had talked about finding things to do at the weekend that were for my heart space, not my head space. Because I am task-oriented, weekends are taken up doing things – chores, cutting the grass, shopping for something specific. It was all about keeping busy and getting stuff done. I needed to find something for my heart: something I enjoyed doing that would fill my time, bring some pleasure as well as heal the pain. I'm slowly getting back into wine tasting and cooking, but it's not enough. At an event for Evie's Gift, Patsy had a brain-wave; why not do a photography course? I loved taking photographs before Evie fell ill, and I wasn't too bad at it either. So that's where I'm going next, to track down a course locally that can help me do something creative that I used to love. I had given Evie my old Nikon D3000 and was teaching her to use it, so now I could get back into that groove. By paying more attention to the 'heart space', I would hopefully improve at work.

I'm the CEO of a charity, and my trustees were amazing during Evie's illness and after her death. They had sat back and let me do things at my own pace and rolled with the punches when I had the down days. Now, nearly two years down the line, they are still great but I sense that they don't really understand. Their life experiences haven't given them the insight into my world, and that is a good thing because I wouldn't wish this on anyone. I am, without doubt, hugely indebted to them for their patience, but like so many other 'muggle' parents, they just don't understand, and I pray that they never will.

Patsy's time back at work has been a very different experience. The first few weeks and months were okay, but after a while she started to get the sense that they simply didn't want the woman who cries unexpectedly in their team. This has to be balanced by the fact that we are probably overly sensitive to criticism, and see demons at every turn. But even so, the way that she was treated got worse over time. Colleagues would tell tales to the partners, others would criticise her work publicly, and they couldn't grasp that the grief affects you in unimaginable ways. Work, instead of being a place of sanctuary became a place of pain. She was just replacing one pain with another. I told her that she should leave, take another job anywhere else doing anything rather than putting up with people who didn't understand. She felt that she'd never find another job that paid as well, but I simply didn't care. I wanted my grieving wife to be pain-free for at least part of every day. We weren't paying for Evie's school fees anymore and so money was less of a pressure. What she will do I have no idea at present, but if she leaves, then I will be a lot happier. We have lost our child, our future, and part of ourselves, and are still here putting one foot in front of the other, so we can deal with anything. Again, Evie's death shows us what is important.

Employers across the country face bereaved parents every day, and their reactions form an enormous spectrum from the good to the bad and the downright ugly. But we always come back to the point that, because they haven't experienced it, they don't know what it feels like and what to expect from us. Eventually, they will all start asking: when will you move on? When will you get back to normal? We won't. **Ever**. We will adapt, we will get better at keeping the mask up, and will be able to do so for longer each day. But we won't move on, because part of us is dead along with our child.

Chapter 11

The Evolution of Grief

At just 18 months into this new world of ours, I can already see differences in how we feel compared to last year. Year one wasn't quite 'shock and awe' but it wasn't far off. Our priorities are changing, our grief is changing. Different things have become important now, and as many others have become trivial. Pain and loss force you to focus on what matters. Once you have made the decision to carry on living, then the energy that you have must go into achieving a life that is **worth** living. In the first few months after Evie's death I felt true despair, a hole in my life that I thought no-one and nothing could fill. It was almost unbearable. On four separate occasions I was seconds away from joining her. It's not something I have spoken about publicly before, and I will probably avoid discussing it if asked. Suffice to say that I'm still here and have decided to make my life as pain-free as possible. I have learned what is truly important and matters. Evie's memory matters. Patsy matters. Family matters. Money is just that: money. A career is a means to an end. A house is a roof and four walls with stuff inside. Loving those around you, and being loved by them in return, is everything.

In the early days, the despair was overwhelming and many other bereaved parents told me that over time you get used to carrying the pain. I think they may be right, but I would add that you just get used to it. Now, 18 months in, I mostly feel a deep, deep sadness, but not despair. The lows, when they come, can be dark and painful, but I know that I will emerge on the other side because I have experienced it so many times. I still hate the platitudes and meaningless rubbish that people trot out when they can't think what to say. I still resent the cowards that abandoned Evie when she needed them. Will I forgive them? Probably not, but now I just don't care about them. They aren't worth wasting oxygen on. They are outweighed by a few golden friends who care.

I have lost my daughter, so now I have to focus every ounce of strength and energy on those closest to me that I love dearly. In some ways it is selfish, because I am trying to convince myself that I can still help people, and I also need to generate that same love in return. Without it, what purpose is there? Why carry on?

The supposed 'grief journey' that so-called experts have devised offers thoughts and ideas, but little more. Nothing in life is that predictable or linear. My emotions still bounce around all over the place. Unexpected crashes come and go, but that's just part of my new life. My newly-bereaved parent life – a phrase that I never thought I would have to utter. I still cry at the thought of Evie's death, though it is less frequent now. The evolution of grief is no different from anything else: it is unpredictable, volatile, and painful. But it is an evolution and definitely not a revolution. Am I better at 'carrying the grief'? I don't know, but I can function for longer, keep the mask up for longer. I can hide from the pain for longer. If I give in to it, or don't have the strength to hold it back, it can still be savage even now.

My patience has been tested many times over the last few months, and now I am less tolerant of those that have no grasp of the pain that I feel. When my wife's senior partner at work wrote to her and told her that the days when she was upset over Evie's death were 'a corrupting influence in an otherwise happy workplace', the final straw broke the proverbial camel's back. Initially I was stunned that someone could be so callous, but then I realised that Patsy's health was far more important. The message, I suppose, is that money isn't important. Loving your wife, as much happiness as you can muster, and surviving are important.

After 18 months of life without Evie I have also learned that I need to look after myself if I am to be of any use to others. I have learned to say 'no' when asked to take on more work. I have learned to offload work to others and stop beating myself up when things don't go the way I want. The exhaustion that comes with losing your child means that you can't work as effectively as before, no matter how hard you might try. Your brain isn't as quick, you forget everything, and as work builds up even the most confident person can feel overwhelmed. I can throw time, energy, and effort at a problem and still make a right royal mess of it. It has been a valuable lesson to learn. A salutary lesson.

As the rawness of the pain subsides a little and you become used to living with it, so you also develop more capacity to understand what is happening to you. I found that I wanted to understand what I was doing and why. I wanted to know how I had got to the emotional place that I was now experiencing. I wanted to know why I felt so vulnerable. Only time can give you back that mental capacity, as you release the energy being used up by grieving. Once you understand what you are thinking, you can figure out if you care about it or not. You can figure out if you can be bothered to try and tackle it. As an example, right now in late July 2019, I am experiencing flashbacks again; a symptom of PTSD. A discussion with my counsellor highlighted that so long as they weren't intruding on my ability to function there was no need to worry, but should they become difficult to cope with, or more frequent, then I would need to learn to manage them. We talked about why I was seeing that first moment in Spain when the neurosurgeon told us that Evie had a brain tumour. Why was it so important? What happened in that moment that had become important now? Or was it just that the original raw pain had moved to the background of my mind, leaving other moments to become more apparent? I don't have an answer yet. We are still exploring it, but at least I have the brain power to think about it without crumbling.

While my own grief was evolving, so was Patsy's, but in a completely different way. It is almost as if she is about six months behind me. Grief doesn't follow the same route for us, but I am recognising things and feelings in her that I went through months ago. It isn't a race to see who gets somewhere first, but it is upsetting to witness those feelings in someone else. The main point though is that, now I have stopped trying to fix her, the tension between us has subsided. Moreover, she has gone through things that have passed me by. I don't know if my grief will include them later or not at all. Patsy seemed more static in her grief, it changed less. It was unending, overwhelming pain for so long.

One of the toughest things about evolving grief is that you've no idea what is coming and when, so you can't prepare. My experience in the RAF of dealing with sudden issues or crises has given me the ability to roll with it a little and cope when something strikes, but I'd like to have an idea of what to expect. The trouble is that, because grief is so different for everyone, no-one can tell me what's next. There are dozens of books out there showing lovely graphs or curves of the 'grief journey'. While sometimes I think that it might be helpful to at least identify the elements that I haven't experienced yet, part of me doesn't want to know. I also get angry when some PhD who lost their cat has decided that they are an expert and thinks that they can map it out. What a load of crap. Grief for us has been impossible to map out for a day, let alone a number of years. I know that the coming years will bounce about all over the place, with sudden and short-term problems as well as steady transitions. But I also now 'know' that there will be a gentle progression towards a new life where I'll feel able to survive and exist in a world where I can cope with the pain. It might be that I never stop taking anti-depressants, and if that's the case then I can live with that. One successful evolution is that I no longer beat myself up over failing to succeed. Not that coming off anti-depressants is success as such, but it is a sort of goal. Importantly though, it isn't something to fall on your sword over.

Chapter 12

A New Life: A New 'Normal'

'The exclusive club that no-one wants to belong to', is how we have heard the world of bereaved parents described. It sums it up pretty well. Everything has changed. All the usual parameters of what is important and what isn't have gone. Almost every 'norm' that I once knew no longer applies. There are massive emotional changes as well as physical ones. Our financial position changed almost immediately as we were no longer paying school fees. Suddenly we could afford to do things, but they are things that we simply don't want to do. Why would we want to go out to dinner without Evie? She loved food, and taking her out was a real pleasure because she enjoyed it so much. Why book a holiday without her? And when we did do these things, we felt horribly guilty because the only reason that we could afford them was because Evie wasn't here. Early on we would go out for the day, and then rush home because when Evie was alive she was permanently hungry, so if we weren't home by 6:30 pm to get her dinner ready she would be eating the furniture. Now we didn't need to rush back because it was just us, and we could eat whenever we felt like it. It took a long time to get out of that habit.

At the weekends, Evie would always rush into our bedroom at about 7:30 am and clamber into bed in between us. We'd just muck about for a while, have a coffee then get up. Now those Saturday and Sunday mornings are quiet, no noise. We still have a coffee but we get up quickly because the room feels empty without Evie there to liven it up a bit. Patsy has started bell-ringing at a church in Bath, so I get the shopping while she is out. We try and find something to fill the day, as otherwise it would feel empty too. For a long time, I was working at the weekends, partly to prove to myself I could achieve something and partly because I needed to catch up on time lost in the week. That just compounded the exhaustion problem, as I never switched off.

We knew that we needed a holiday, a solid two weeks away from work to rest and just 'be' together. But every time I got close to the point of hitting 'book now' on the internet I couldn't do it. The prospect of going away without Evie was too much. We have gone on short breaks and realised the benefits of resting, but a holiday was too much. Guilt. I have sat back and thought about how many meals out we have eaten after she died, and realised that we just didn't want to be at home because home is where she died. And it feels so empty and quiet without her. We have had a few short breaks of four or five days, and each time we have told ourselves that if we get there and can't cope, we can just come back home again. Each time, we have stayed and been glad that we did. We've rested and got some energy back. Not having to get up at 6 am makes a huge difference. But there was always the same crash when we arrived back home as the realisation that Evie wasn't there was made obvious once again. It's not that we pretended she was still alive while we were away, it was just that it wasn't so blatantly obvious that she was dead. I think we have now reached a position where we recognise that the gain from the rest outweighs the pain of coming home again. I still haven't booked a proper holiday though. I will. Soon. Probably.

Work has changed the most. Before, it was there to generate the money to give Evie the very best start in life that we could manage, to show her so many places and things. To travel, take her to concerts, pay for school trips. Now work is a place for thinking about something else for a while to give the pain a rest. We have a unique freedom now that we don't want. We can go or do what we want, when we want. What's the point of having money when you can't spend it on your daughter?

My new 'normal' life starts in exactly the same way each day. I wake up and, for a fraction of a second, I am blissfully unaware of Evie's loss, then the realisation strikes. I say "Good morning, Pickle," and get up. The energy washes out of me and I feel completely empty, exhausted, and alone. Slowly, while getting showered, I gather what strength I have left and start the day. Work starts to take over my thoughts and I push forward into the day. I put the mask on, adjust it, and face the world. I hit the day running, I'm online and working by 6:30, working at a pretty frantic pace until early afternoon when I realise that I am wiped out again, just like yesterday. The mistakes are creeping in – unforced errors – I forget things. My short-term memory is terrible. I have to write things down straight away or I will forget them. Then I forget to look at the list or can't find it. I take an extended tea break to recover some capacity, it might be an hour or maybe even more. Most days I work into the evening on and off, just to catch up on what I have missed during the afternoon. I'm not trying to prove anything, just keep my head above water to keep that feeling of being overwhelmed at bay. When we hit a busy patch at work, and I can see the tasks building up, I feel that I can't cope; it's all too much. I have to stop, make a coffee, then come back to it again. Each time that happens, I have it sorted fairly quickly and can relax again, but that doesn't stop the feeling of panic striking again the next time it happens. On average I will most likely lose my temper half a dozen times during the day, almost always over something utterly trivial. I will shout and swear at the computer, the printer, or whatever happens to be in range. Sometimes, inevitably it can also be 'whoever' is in range.

Finally, around 10:30, we will go to bed. I say, "Goodnight, Pickle," and there will be a blissful six or seven hours with no pain because I'm asleep. The alarm goes off at 6:05 and it all starts again. Evie never leaves my thoughts during the day. Her image, her voice, her presence is always there no matter what. I'm losing 25%

of my brain power all the time because it is thinking about her, her cancer, and her death. It never ever leaves me. But I battle through it every day.

My first reaction back in February 2018 after Evie died was to run away and leave all the pain behind. Sell the house and move, change jobs. But I didn't, even though the urge was incredibly strong. Several people told us that we should avoid major life-changing decisions because once they are done, they cannot be undone. So, we stayed put. Looking back, I think that was the right decision for us because Evie grew up here: it was the only house she knew and although painful sometimes, the house is full of memories, lovely memories. But it is full of pain too, and I struggle to be in the dining room because we had to turn it into a bedroom for her when she came home. She died in that room. The walls are still covered with the pictures and 'get well' cards from the dozens of people that came to see her. But it is a room of death for me. I pass through it quickly rather than linger. Strangely, I can sit in her bedroom far more easily, and talk to her in there.

Some of the things that I used to enjoy faded into the background. I loved photography, wine, cooking, and holidays, and all have lost their attraction. But slowly, very slowly, some of them are coming back. I prefer to eat dinner in the lounge with a tray on my lap. I have been teaching Leo, one of Evie's lovely friends from senior school, how to cook. I don't think her mother, Sally, will mind me saying that cooking isn't something that she enjoys, so teaching Leo to cook wasn't realistic. Leo listens and learns and it gives me the pleasure of watching as someone learns a skill. There have been times when I have wanted to cancel the lessons because I've felt grotty, but I have managed to break through it and keep going. It's also just nice to have a young person in the house again. And in a strange way it maintains contact with Evie through her friend.

Patsy says that what we are living, or enduring, isn't a life, it's an existence, and she's right. It's an existence that we don't want. It is hard to take pleasure in anything and when you do, the guilt slams into you like a wall. It is a life that I would gladly swap to bring Evie back to Patsy so that she could live out her life as was intended. This is our new life though, and there isn't an alternative. As the saying goes, 'You can run, but you can't hide'. My job now is to fight to preserve her name and her memory as every bereaved parent does. I want a permanent, lasting memory for her. She wrote in a piece of Latin homework that as long as someone remembers you, you aren't truly dead. My role now is to find that permanence in whatever form it might take. We've done a number of things, but I haven't found that perfect result yet. Maybe in some small way, writing this book will help to achieve that. Maybe not. I just know that I am not going to rest until I find it.

One of the hardest parts of our new life, the new normal, is that it is almost having to start off afresh; I imagine it's a bit like when you emigrate, except everything and everyone is the same. You still live in the same place and know the same people, but the way you interact with them all is completely different. It is the weirdest feeling. We look at all of the familiar places and people in a completely different light. When we meet our friends, we are tense, wondering how they are going to react. Will they ignore us? Will they listen? When we are introduced to new people we are braced for the inevitable question, "Do you have any children?" Everything is familiar yet unknown.

But without doubt the thing about our new life that has caught me out the most is the isolation. Everyone else has moved on, got on with their lives. The summer holidays are terrible. People are away on holiday and focused on their own kids and we are left alone with each other. The isolation makes you even less motivated to do anything and the whole package becomes a vicious spiral. It's almost a self-fulfilling prophecy. Many friends are away on holiday, so you become inward-looking, which means that you don't feel like going out when you are invited, so people don't invite you, so you feel isolated and don't feel like going out. So, it goes on. Depression is hard enough to deal with when you are supported; it's nearly impossible to do it alone. We know that we can't expect people to stop going away, so we just dig in for the long term and wait it out. It's a major fight to find the energy to keep going, to make the effort to contact others. But I have to do it.

Throughout this new life there is a constant battle going on between the rational and emotional parts of my brain. Each gains the upper hand for a while, and then it flips again. I know that I have the strength to work, to figure things out and overcome whatever trial is before me, but equally, the emotional trauma means that the fear can take over at will and tip me back into the darkness. As time has gone on, the rational side of my brain gains the upper hand more, which I suppose is good. But when the darkness comes it is always sudden and unexpected. I can sit and listen to Patsy talk about her pain and be completely detached, able to rationalise the problem and think of potential solutions. Then, when the same things happen to me, I haven't got the faintest clue what to do. I am learning slowly that I have to take advantage of the rational periods, and crack on with those jobs that I have put off, otherwise they won't get done.

The analogy that I use to explain this new world is that it's like dropping three stones into a pool of water. The ripples from each interact with the ripples from the other stones. Sometimes, the peaks come together and magnify their effect into an almost normal day. Sometimes the troughs come together and the lows can be deep, and sometimes the effects cancel each other out. What you have is a completely unpredictable confusion of peaks and troughs of different sizes. You can't see what is coming or prepare yourself. You just bob about, spinning. Then someone picks up a dirty great boulder and throws it into the middle.

When Evie was alive, we had our lives mapped out, retirement plans made. We knew where we were going and when. When Patsy's mum and dad died in 2014 we used her share of their inheritance to buy a house in Wales, which we are using as a holiday home. We planned to retire there when Evie left home. All was good. Life's ups and downs came and went, and we were a tight little family unit doing everything together. Now the plans are gone and we can't rewrite them. I for one could never leave Evie now so while we might move house, we will stay close to her. We are reactive, not pro-active. We have learned to adapt, to learn fast. We have also learned that we have to look after ourselves, to be selfish sometimes. Because if we don't, the alternative isn't pleasant.

Chapter 13

Wednesday 'Wisdom' or the Lack Thereof

What follows is a collection of Wednesday Wisdoms that I have written, firstly for The Compassionate Friends Facebook page, and latterly for the Evie's Gift page too. I hope that you don't think the name is arrogant. It was simply lifted from Twitter; it could just as easily have been called Thursday Thoughts. As I said, I started posting them on the Evie's Gift page too because I felt that friends and family needed to get a better grasp of what we were going through: how we felt and what we were thinking, why we would cancel something at the last minute. In a way, I wanted to explain why we were behaving the way we were. Like us in the early days, they had no clue about what it felt like. To be honest I was also sick and tired of some of the platitudes and crass comments that were coming our way, and wanted to do something about it. Some of the WWs were written or tweaked deliberately with friends in mind because we spend so much time wearing a mask that most of them have absolutely no clue of what is happening to us. Let's not beat about the bush – neither of us want to be on this Earth without Evie, so being told that we are so strong and how 'proud' of us Evie would be gets seriously irritating at times. I also wanted to let friends know that they don't have to walk on eggshells around us and that anyone who is avoiding talking about Evie because they thought it would hurt us, was barking up the wrong tree. All bereaved parents need to talk about their children. As I have said time and again (and sadly little has changed), by avoiding talk of Evie, they are lobbing out the biggest insult. This world of ours is full of myths and misunderstandings. People make broad assumptions based on …. well, based on nothing more than guesswork to be honest, and most of the time they are completely wrong. So wrong, in fact, it makes me angry. How can people be that stupid? Because they've never experienced it or anything like it. I felt that I had a duty to do something about that ignorance. To educate.

This chapter is Chapter 13 for a reason; Evie was ill for 13 weeks, and she was 13 when she died. We now actively seek out table 13 at restaurants and so on, just to thumb our nose at the world or fate, but that's another story entirely.

I have found writing the WWs extremely helpful. As I write each one, I am forced to think about what I am writing, questioning myself about how honest I am being and what I am trying to get across. By doing that, I process the thoughts, dig deeper, and it helps me come to terms with that particular problem or issue. Or at least admit that it exists. But I also think about how the reader will interpret the words. Is it clear? Is it unambiguous? The process of picking a topic makes me face the hard questions, and while that hurts sometimes, it keeps me honest with myself. So many times, I have answered questions from friends with the words that they want to hear, or I have held back for fear of upsetting others. Ironic really. The writing is totally honest, almost brutal on occasion. It is from the heart and I don't hold anything back. I do moderate my language though as, on occasion, my rage at certain things might not be best expressed in its fullest force!

The following Wednesday Wisdoms are all a reflection on my personal experiences. They are not informed by medical research, they have not been canvassed from other bereaved parents, nor do they necessarily even reflect Patsy's view. They are just me dumping my brain onto a piece of paper. They aren't meant to be taken as advice or guidance either, so please don't get in touch saying that x, y, or z didn't work for you. As always, everyone grieves in a different way, so you have to tread your own path. You may disagree entirely with everything that I have written, and that's fine too. Your grief is your grief, not mine. So now that I have got the caveats out of the way, here they are. Make of them what you will.

31 Jan 19

"Be kind to yourself" – how many times have we all been told that? But what does it actually mean? I struggled with that question for months until it finally dawned on me. Losing Evie felt like failure – I had failed to keep her alive, even though there was absolutely nothing I could have done to prevent her cancer or her death. To compensate I threw myself into work in an effort to prove to myself that I could still achieve something despite this dreadful loss. Of course, I wasn't achieving much at work either because I couldn't focus.

I learned to accept that I wasn't going to be functioning at 100% for some time, and not to get frustrated or angry with myself for missing targets and so on, because quite simply, NOTHING else mattered. Evie was gone and, in comparison, everything else was trivia. "Be kind to yourself" meant don't give yourself a hard time for grieving and struggling to survive. Accept that sometimes things take longer or don't work out. That there are sufficient frustrations in this world without giving yourself a hard time over something you can't control.

6 Feb 19

Let yourself enjoy things. If you are anything like me, there is a 'noise' in your head constantly, thoughts of our children whirling around in a 'white noise' that soaks up energy and capacity to think. It's exhausting. After Evie died I forgot to do the things I loved: cooking, baking, and enjoying a decent glass of wine. I felt guilty if I enjoyed something because Evie wasn't there to share it. But you know, I believe that we need to enjoy things, if only for a short while. Just doing something for ourselves, something that we once loved gives our brains a respite from the pain, allowing it to heal, recover, and, as importantly, rest.

It takes enormous energy and drive to force ourselves to sit and read, knit, cook something interesting, or spend an hour on that hobby that once gave us pleasure. But we MUST do it. I'm now cooking again, and am teaching one of Evie's best friends to cook. Yes it's sad, but it's also productive. For a couple of hours each month, the noise in my head subsides a little and my blood pressure drops. Evie isn't there, but if I'm not fit and healthy then I can't work to preserve her memory.

If we look after ourselves, we can do more to make certain that our children's names are remembered by those around us.

13 Feb 19

Fresh air and exercise. Not for one minute am I suggesting that you climb Everest or run a marathon, but simply getting out and about does seem to bring benefits. Finding something that helps you to deal with grief in any way is always something that we seek. I walk long distances. I have done long distance walks for a few years now, but recently walking has taken on a new purpose. Last October I walked 175 miles in 7 days around the Cornish coast – averaging 26 miles a day with 6,000 feet of climb a day, burning 5,500+ calories each day. I did it as a fundraiser but I have found walking just 6 or 8 miles on my own to be incredibly therapeutic.

When I am walking my mind relaxes and just wanders. Thoughts about Evie come and go, I smile, I cry, I think about work or home or Evie's Gift. But somehow, I don't dwell on anything. I notice what is happening around me. The wildlife and the trees and fields. I say 'hello' to total strangers.

My wife and I do walk together but she wants to stroll and I want to power up, load the backpack and speed off, so mostly the bigger walks are on my own. I can set my own pace, stop as and when I feel like it, and talk softly to Evie as I go along. I don't know why it helps but it does seem to. Endorphins? Proximity to God's creations? Or just the mechanical repetition of walking. My bereavement counsellor once said that she believed it was because the left and right sides of the brain are working alternately to move my limbs and that helps me to process the grief. I don't actually care about the how or why it works, because for me it does work, and that is what counts. For a couple of hours each walk, the world is a nicer, more bearable, place.

Get the walking boots out and hit the hills!

20 Feb 19

Music has the power to communicate in a way that words cannot. I have found that music can lift a mood as well as remind you of what is lost. Some of the songs that Evie loved are bright and breezy but too painful to listen to, others reflect a feeling or memory so closely that they just seem right. Of course, finding those ones that can lift your mood is hard and can involve stumbling over a lot of pain along the way.

At Evie's Celebration of Life we played 'Stay a Little Longer' by Brothers Osborne, a rock-country song that for a few months after her death I found difficult to listen to, but now its fabulous guitar riff reminds me of how vibrant

Evie was. ELO's 'Mr Blue Sky' makes me smile every time I listen to it. Evie's own music choices, all of which are on my iPhone, are there showing what she loved to listen to and I play them a lot. In some strange way it's a link straight to her and what she liked. Like all things, music can be a double-edged sword, as we found last week when we saw Ward Thomas, one of her favourite country bands. The music was great but it was just wrong that Evie wasn't there with us.

If you can find music that lifts the soul then you have a refuge. For me I can lose myself in 'Va Tosca', an aria from Puccini's Tosca, sung by Tito Gobbi (sadly only in mono) who delivers a song of such chilling malevolence as the evil police chief Scarpia, that no-one has matched it since. A strange choice perhaps, but the power of the music communicates in a way that words can only dream of.

As bereaved parents, our comforts can come in three-minute musical packages, and that for me is just fine.

27 Feb 19

Finding a reason to carry on after the loss of a child is something that dogs all of us, finding a purpose once again, a reason to be here. Look around you – so many parents who have lost children have set up charities in their child's name, or fundraise on behalf of a cause, or research into the disease that took their child. Why? For me, at face value, there are two very simple reasons; firstly, to make sure that Evie's name lives on long after I have died, and secondly, because we spotted a need that no other charity was filling. But underneath that was a far more fundamental need: a need to help, be needed, to regain that purpose in life once again, or at least something towards that goal.

Setting up a charity is a pretty extreme step to take and it takes a lot of time and energy, and there are so many other ways that you can help others. Fundraise for a charity that has been involved with you, look out for elderly neighbours, do a beach clean looking for plastic, do litter picks or volunteer your time for any one of 167,000 charities that are active in the UK. It's one of those dreadful clichés to say it's 'giving something back', but the act of selflessness does help us through a dark time. It makes us feel valued. For me, being needed is central to who I am, who I want to be. On Christmas Day we volunteered for Bath Churches Open Christmas pretty much all day, serving a Christmas meal to people living alone and those who are homeless. The gain for us was that we didn't have to think about Evie not being there for our first Christmas without her, we just got on with the job, and then went home to chicken fajitas and a decent bottle of wine. It was like a normal Saturday night with better stuff on TV.

Even more simply, Evie helped others all the time, so I owe it to her to continue that legacy. Whatever you do, helping someone or something else will give you a lift, so why not give it a go? It doesn't have to be much, and whatever you choose to do for someone else, it will feel good.

6 Mar 19

"How do you make a headache go away?" It was one of my dad's favourite sayings. The answer was, "Stopping banging your head against the wall." In modern language, I suppose, you might say, "Don't sweat the small stuff." In our lives as bereaved parents, we have enough to worry about without us taking on things we can't influence.

One of the classic problems that we all face is the one where everyone else seems to move on with their lives while we are stuck in some weird time warp, the worst kind of groundhog day, reliving the nightmare of our child's death. But you know what, those old friends getting on with their lives is inevitable, and we can't do anything to stop it. As much as they love us, and care about our pain, we cannot expect them to stop in their tracks as we have. The more we let it bother us, the more it hurts.

Accept that we can't stop it happening and things become easier. In other words, "stop banging your head against the 'friends' wall", and the headache goes away.

Instead, direct your energy into areas that you can influence. Make time for yourself, find ways to preserve your child's memory or maybe just rest. Some things cannot be changed, so maybe we should learn to recognise them and influence rather than try to change? And of course, take it slowly with small steps along the way. It isn't easy, but it's less painful than a headache for a lifetime.

13 Mar 19

"Let me know if there's anything I can do." Probably the phrase that all of us have heard, spoken with the very best of intentions, and the one that rings the hollowest. Our world as a bereaved parent has been shattered, finding the motivation to get up some days can be hard enough without sitting down to think 'Now, Johnny said he'd help, what can I ask him to do?' So, we don't ask. And things don't get done. And the vicious spiral continues because people stop offering. Social isolation is one of our biggest enemies. And yet we need help in so many ways. A true friend does those little things without being asked, they just turn up to take you out for a coffee, they bring a meal to save you the effort of cooking, or they just collect your wheelie bin and bring it back. All without fanfare. Friends like that keep us from the edge.

As we all know, our address books have changed beyond all recognition. People or family that were once close are now strangers; don't forget that losing a child is a kind of leprosy and might be contagious! I'm being sarcastic of course, but that's how it feels. So how can we overcome this malaise? In a word, **ask**. Ask for help, ask people to do the chores that we don't have the energy to do. Call THEM and suggest a coffee. It is my belief that the majority of these 'call me' offers are genuine, so take advantage of them.

We don't have to go through this experience alone, and we certainly don't have to isolate ourselves from the world. Our British tendency is to wade through it all, stoically tackling every little problem that comes along on our own. But there are dozens of 'willing' volunteers out there who can help, so push pride or stoicism aside and ask for help. If you can't do it face to face, then text or email, though it is much harder for people to turn you down to your face! For the insincere offers, and there will be some, you'll know where you stand and can score that name off your Christmas card list (ours has reduced by about 50%!). For the rest, they will be glad that you've opened the door and they can do something to help. Most of our friends haven't got the faintest idea what to say or do, so they keep quiet, fearing that they might say the wrong thing or upset us. They say, "We thought that we would leave you in peace," or "We thought that you wouldn't want visitors." What they don't realise – and why should they? – is that what we hear is, *"We're uncomfortable seeing you in pain so we'll pretend that you are doing fine and don't need us."* They don't realise that their absence causes yet more pain. So, take that first step and ask for help, suggest a coffee; break the mould and take the opportunity to talk about your child at the same time. In an ideal world you shouldn't have to, but we live in an imperfect world where our sense of community has died. Be the bigger person and take the first step.

If all else fails, your new friends in the bereaved parent community will ALWAYS be there for you, because they are living the same life.

20 Mar 19

A sense of direction. Seems straightforward doesn't it? But for me, losing Evie left me feeling adrift, almost becalmed. I completely lost any sense of direction. Work was pointless, life was pointless. Our job as parents was to bring Evie up and prepare her for adulthood. We had a marker in the sand out in the distance, set at Evie being 18,

21, or whenever she finished full-time education or moved out to live her own life. We might have meandered about a bit along the way, but we knew which general direction to go in. Our role in life was to give her the tools that she needed to become a good person and play her part in the world. When Evie died it felt as if someone had ripped that marker out and had thrown it away, put a bag on my head, spun me round and round, then turned the lights off and said, "Off you go!" I had absolutely no idea which way to go. I was lost, literally and figuratively.

It took many months of counselling to even recognise this was what was going on. The groundhog day of just existing was all I knew. Get up, eat, work, sleep, repeat. Without direction we wander and achieve little. So, I decided to set an artificial goal, created a new 'marker in the sand' a few months out just to give me something to point at. For me it was creating a number of things that would preserve Evie's memory once I had died. Her headstone, the charity Evie's Gift. It was a short-term goal and I've now more or less passed it and am pointing at another goal a couple of years away: to make Evie's Gift financially sustainable in the long term. It's not a personal 'life goal' as I'm not ready to figure out what that might be, but it provides me with a something to think about. A direction of sorts. When I get there, with a bit of luck and a following wind, I'll be able to set a new one five or more years out and maybe I'll have a 'life goal' too. Or I might just set another short-term one if I'm not ready. For now though, it's still baby steps, but at least they're steps heading in a direction.

Goals can be anything – managing a full weekly shop at Tesco, going back to work, taking the decision on what headstone to choose or just getting through the day without screaming at someone. They can be a day away, a month or a year, whatever you feel capable of. But they should be **achievable**. Don't set yourself a target that you can fail to reach because that will just reinforce all the tough times. Goals and targets, for me, give back a sense of direction, and because of the type of person I am I need that to keep my head straight.

27 Mar 19

When Evie was born, I decided to start buying wines from her birth year, 2004. I planned to build a collection over the years and then, when she was old enough, hand over some of them for her to either drink and enjoy, or sell, as they should have increased in value significantly by then. Evie loved food and so, for me, teaching her about matching food and wine was a natural next step once she was old enough to drink. I looked forward to seeing her explore the world of wine and understand that it can be a fascinating experience, matching the flavours and textures with food.

When she died, I was sat looking at about 300 bottles that no longer held any meaning. They were no longer fabulous bottles of enjoyment, but had become a red, white, or bubbly liquid in a bottle, nothing more. My favourite hobby had died with Evie. I had collected everything from good value stuff at £6-8 a bottle, right up to wine from some of the best producers in the world. As Evie had grown up, we had drunk some beautiful wines from 2004 to celebrate her birthday or at Christmas. Now what was the point? My initial reaction was to dump the whole lot into the auction market and be rid of it. Evie was gone, so the connection and emotional value of the wine was gone too. But ... I sat on my hands. I did that for two reasons; firstly, I had no motivation to do anything, and quite frankly I couldn't be bothered, and secondly, because someone had said, "Don't decide anything quickly." Once done, a lot of things can't be undone.

Then as we approached Evie's birthday in September last year, our first without her, it popped into my head that we would normally have opened a decent bottle of wine from 2004 to mark the day. We had already invited some of her friends and their parents over to share her favourite meal: steak, chips, and carrots with a raspberry pavlova. So, I opened the 2004s for the parents. At that point, I remembered that wine is for sharing with friends: it isn't a commodity like copper or oil. That started me thinking about the rest of the collection. Wine is a living, breathing thing and it ages and evolves with time, just like people. The wine was getting older even though Evie was forever 13. It was a way of staying in touch with her.

So now I'm keeping the wine. I'll open a straightforward 2004 when I want to share something that was picked and pressed within a few days of her birth. I'll open one of those special bottles when I want to remember how special she was. The better bottles will still be alive and kicking long after I've left this earth, so in a way she's living beyond me, which is as it should be.

A few bottles of wine have taught me that you should never act in haste, because once things are gone, it's bloody hard to get them back. It's also taught me that you can find connections to your child in the strangest ways, but that strangeness doesn't matter, because any connection is good.

3 Apr 19
The pain never goes away, you never 'get over it' or 'move on'. The loss of a child, no matter how old they were, is a devastating experience that we never 'get over'. A lot of the 'muggles' out there treat the death of a child in the same way that they would the loss of a parent, friend, or relative, as they don't know any different. And I pray that they never will. They think that you will eventually move on and are surprised when you don't. A few years ago we lost both of Patsy's parents within a period of five days and the pain was enormous. I'd known them since I was 12 years old and it hurt as much as losing my own father. Evie's death was a thousand times worse, believe

me, but many people cannot grasp that fact because they haven't experienced it. Honestly, the next person that tells me that 'they understand' because their pet or horse died is going to regret it. Losing your dogs, cats, horses – they are mostly definitely NOT the same as losing a child, so don't insult me. Dealing with people who think that way is difficult because I want to rage at them, but that won't solve anything. It only serves to raise my blood pressure, which is bad enough as it is.

When Evie died, one of the nurses that was looking after her talked to me about the various stages of grief; 'anger' is definitely a stage and I'm definitely in it right now. That said, grief isn't a linear process. It's far too unpredictable, but that's a subject for another day. Lisa, the Julia's House Hospice nurse, talked to me about how to express what I was feeling so my brain could 'process it' – by the way, I'm never quite sure what 'process' means! One of the things that she suggested was to write it down. Maybe keep a daily journal, noting down anything and everything that I felt, how bad things were, what upset me, or what lifted me, however briefly. I've never been one for diaries or journals, so that was a non-starter. But I did start to write things. Don't laugh, but I wrote poetry. I've spent my 54 years hating poetry, finding it very difficult to understand and completely lacking in sense. All a load of flowery stuff and nonsense. But I wrote. I could be driving or watching TV and a word or phrase about Evie or what had happened to her or us would pop into my head. I'd stop what I was doing and let the words flow. I don't force it, and I only write when something resonates. I think I may have sent one to The Compassionate Friends for inclusion in a newsletter, but in the main they are for internal consumption only; primarily because they aren't very good. Okay, they're rubbish, but who cares? Evie had the writing gene in this family, as is shown very clearly by her book 'Written by the Stars'.

I have no idea if writing these thoughts down has helped me 'process' anything, but looking back at them now you can see a gradual progression from the abyss of loss, to a call for help, and then anger. And now of course, I am writing 'Wednesday Wisdom'. I don't think for one second that what I scribble down is wise in any sense, but it helps me understand what is happening in my head, and from a completely selfish perspective that is its purpose. I know of people who write diaries, and Maria, one of the Trustees at TCF, writes a 'conversation' between herself and her son every week and publishes it on FB. It doesn't matter what form your writing takes, just give it a go. Do it publicly, or keep it private, it doesn't matter. I find that writing it down, re-reading it, and then thinking about it helps me to understand what I am thinking and feeling and why. All I have to do now is figure out what I do with that knowledge about myself! Answers on a postcard please.

10 Apr 19

One of the things that I find helpful is walking. Not a stroll to the shops, or walking the dog for 20 minutes (we don't have a dog), but a day-long, 20-mile hike on my own. After 15 months without Evie, it is the one and only time when my mind quietens and the pain subsides enough for me to relax. I don't stop very much, only for short snack or wee breaks, I just keeping ploughing on. Evie wanders into my mind and we have a chat and she wanders out again. Work stresses come and go, and the world passes me by. It is the ONLY time when my mind is vaguely at peace from the pain.

I thought for ages about why that might be so, and came up with all the usual clichés about being in the fresh air, seeing that you are part of something bigger. That may well be true but I don't think that's the answer, at least not for me. I took a mindfulness course a few years ago and that got me somewhere to understanding what might be happening: being 'in the moment'. It took a long discussion with my counsellor to get the answer. Walking means that both sides of the brain are working together to move limbs, control breathing, sight and hearing. Using both halves of your brain in such a way helps you to process complex information more effectively, and so by doing it for extended periods you get to free up brain capacity to think subconsciously about the trauma of loss. In some way your brain is working hyper-efficiently, with few external distractions. Sitting quietly and contemplating your navel doesn't work because most of your brain goes dormant. What the counsellor told me was that any activity that uses both halves of your brain will help; if you prune the roses, grab the stem with one hand and cut with the other. I would imagine that knitting has similar benefits as both hands are working together. The repetitious activity over time is what helps.

The side benefit for me is that walking all day burns calories and keeps the middle age spread at bay a little longer. I do also get to see bits of the countryside that I would otherwise miss. But, most importantly, I get to chat to Evie without feeling like a complete wally. I talk out loud; I ask her advice, I ask for help, I tell her about what's going on. Once when I was walking along the tow path to Bath, doing a quick 18-mile training walk, I was flagging and getting tired. I swear I felt her hands in the small of my back pushing me along gently.

So now, working on the principle that, if 20 miles is good for me then more must be better, I'm doing 24 hours non-stop on 21 June, aiming at hiking 66 miles in one go. It's not a fundraiser, it's just me being selfish, looking for some peace. I'll have a look on Amazon and see if they sell new knees and hips…

17 Apr 19
There's a lot of talk of 'life-changing events' and 'life-changing injuries', but losing a child is a 'person-changing event'. I'm no longer the person that I used to be; so much has changed. We all grieve in different ways, and so it follows that we all change in different ways. Whether or not we accept the person that we have now become or try and go back to the person that we once were, is open to

debate and personal circumstance. I don't know that I want to go back as that would dishonour Evie, as if her loss made no difference. For guidance when I was at Evie's grave recently, I asked her what she thought. I didn't really need an answer because Evie was always happy in her own skin, happy to be herself and not care what others may have thought. I was so proud of her strength of character. I already knew the answer to my question of course, I just needed to be reminded of it. I am who I am, and some people can't deal with the new 'me' anymore. Their loss, "bye, been nice knowing you".

But the changes that happen in us evolve with time too. In the early months following Evie's death, I didn't like the person that I had become. I had no self-confidence, I didn't trust my own decisions, I completely lacked motivation to do anything and felt the slide into depression eating me away. It was corrosive. I was not in control of my emotions, feelings or capabilities and that frightened me. Quite literally, I felt as if I was falling into a bottomless pit. Making things even more complicated is the fact that the person that I have become changes from day to day. Friends want to help, to 'cheer me up' or 'make me better'. But what may work today, almost certainly won't work tomorrow. Patsy and I don't have surviving children, so for those bereaved parents with other children to look after, can they ever be the 'same' parent that these children have grown up with? The same parent that they need?

People frequently ask me how I cope and my standard reply now is "Drugs and alcohol". They look at me unsure if I am joking or not. I'm not. Don't be mistaken, without anti-depressants I don't know where I would be now. They don't work for everyone, but they worked, and still work, for me. They gave me back the capacity to think, they stopped the deepest of the lows. The lows still come, but they aren't as deep and don't last as long. I'm no longer sliding into that bottomless pit and am now, slowly, very slowly, clawing my way back up; up not 'out'. My 'best' day now is probably the equivalent of a pretty poor day before Evie fell ill. A glass or two of wine simply takes the edge off, and for a couple of hours I can hide. We don't actually drink any more than we did before, it just has a different purpose now.

I am most definitely a different person, my views on many things are vastly different. For example, I can say that death no longer holds any fear for me. Shuffling off this mortal coil means I will be with my beautiful daughter again. My world has polarised completely into black and white. At one end of the spectrum there is death, at the other there is everything else, there's nothing in the middle; there's no grey, everything else is trivia. Before Evie was ill, I didn't suffer fools gladly, now I don't suffer them at all. For example, compared to 'muggles', I don't care about Brexit in the least. To me it simply isn't important. But I have also realised something: I have survived and am living through the absolute worst thing that could ever happen to me. If I can survive this, I can survive anything that this world can throw at me. Because at the end of the day, it **cannot** get any worse. It can be added to, but not get worse. Anything else that comes my way isn't a problem, it's no more than a solution that I haven't found yet. Have I accepted who I have become? I don't know. But I do know that I'm not going to try and change who I am because that would imply that losing Evie had no impact on me, and that is quite wrong.

24 Apr 19

We all grieve in different ways. How many times have we all been told that? It is so true, but actually dealing with it is a whole different ball game. Since Evie died, I have met a lot of bereaved parents and seen the full spectrum of emotions and ways of facing grief. The stereotype is that men take their grief, stick it in a box, and bury it. Ignore the pain and try to carry on. I have seen that for certain, but I have also seen many broken men trying to work out what the hell is going on and how they can deal with it; I include myself in that.

For any couple, losing a child places enormous strain on their relationship. Each person is dealing with their own 'private' grief as well as somehow trying to help their partner along the way. It's an almost impossible combination. Watching your wife or husband in pain is horrible: you want to help yet lack the skills and knowledge to do so easily. Because we all grieve in different ways, what works for one won't work for the other, but that is all the knowledge that we have. So, what do you do? If you are waiting for the magic bullet answer, I'm afraid you are going to be disappointed, as I don't have it. And even if I did, it probably wouldn't work for you anyway. The only advice I can give is to listen.

Grief is isolating at the best of times, and the fact that you can't lean on your husband or wife for support as much as you need to makes it worse. Both partners are mired in pain and, in many cases, neither has the energy or brain capacity to do much for the other, especially in the early days. This isn't to say that it is all doom and gloom, far from it. You both know and feel the same pain, which means that you understand and know what it feels like. The trick is to develop a level of patience that you've probably never managed before. To paraphrase the Bible, "Do unto others as you would have them do unto you". You are going to behave and react in unpredictable and irrational ways, so it is perfectly natural that your partner will do the same. How do you want them to react to you? How will you react to them?

To make it all even more complicated, the way that you grieve and what you feel will change over time. Different things will become important or trivial. For me, the early days were a blur. People often ask if I felt numb. I didn't feel numb, I felt devastated, lost, and that feeling of loss was overwhelming. It masked everything else. Now, the blur has gone and the loss has crystalized. It has become more 'real'. The path of grief that Pats and I have followed is different, not faster or slower, just different. And I have no idea how those two paths will develop either, so I can't predict what will happen next. In turn that means that I can't put measures in place to deal with them until they happen. As a bereaved parent you always spend your life on the back foot; always reactive, never pro-active.

Watching someone you love being in pain is incredibly difficult. You feel helpless, when all you want to do is take some of the pain away. You know you can't make it 'better', but taking some pain away for a while might ease things. But sometimes you have to step away a little and see how things develop, avoiding the obvious bear traps. I know that certain things send either of us into a rage. Patsy hates platitudes, especially, "Evie wouldn't want you to be sad/in pain/upset/etc." Evie wouldn't want to be dead either! For me, it is people changing the subject when I talk about Evie. Someone once said to me, "I find it uncomfortable talking about her, so I'd rather not." My rather harsh response was, "You get to feel uncomfortable for three minutes and then go home and forget it, I live with indescribable pain 24 hours a day, 365 days a year, so if you class yourself as a friend, suck it up for three minutes!" The point here is that the thing that winds Patsy up doesn't always bother me, and vice versa. But sometimes it does. Our world is very confused as you can see.

We are all different, and we all grieve in different ways, so I'm afraid that we must be aware of how our partners grieve and learn, quickly, to avoid those bear traps. But we also need to give them space sometimes and learn to listen in a whole new way.

1 May 19

Am I still a dad? Evie was our only child and now she's gone. The three of us were a neat little family unit, now there's just the two of us. So, am I still a dad? No-one calls me Daddy any more, and all of the things that I loved doing as a dad have gone. I wrote a short piece on this subject about 8-10 months ago, so I wondered how my thoughts on it have changed. Unlike many bereaved parents, we don't have other children, so the question has a real resonance for me. I saw myself as Daddy, not Bryan. Being a dad was my identity.

I loved being a dad. I loved doing all those things that dads do with kids: being a dad taxi, making snowmen, playing Scrabble, teaching her to cook, nagging her to do her homework. Pats and I were 40 when Evie was born so had been together as a couple for a very long time before then. Now we are back to being a couple. It's a situation that we don't want and would give anything to reverse. Both of us would gladly swap places with Evie to bring her back to live her life.

So now here I am, back to being a husband again, with all of the trappings of parenthood gone. Evie's things are still here, her room is pretty much as it was when we went on holiday in October 2017. Her photos are everywhere in the house. I talk to her all the time, I listen to her music choices, I watch her DVDs. But she's not here, so I don't feel like a dad. My daily routines and actions don't contain anything that a father would do. There is an enormous void in my life.

I miss the 'daddy-ness' of it all. I miss waiting for her energetic arrival home after school when the first question was always, "What can I have to eat?" The theory is that, yes, of course I am still a dad, I helped bring Evie into this world, but everything that goes with being a dad has gone. Nothing remains. Of all the peripheral impacts of her death, this is the one that I struggle with the most. At counselling, I have talked about it many times and still don't have a solution. I don't even know if there is a solution. It may well be that I can't do anything about it and just have to adapt, but right now I'm not prepared to do that. Unlike other Wednesday Wisdoms, I don't have an answer or 'this has worked for me' point to make. This time, all I can offer is that some problems take longer to work through or come to accept than others. When Evie died, I spent months with my brain racing frantically trying to find the answer to the problem that was her death, trying to find a solution that would bring her back. It drained me of energy because I couldn't turn it off. I'm task-driven, so it made sense to me that her death was just another problem to be solved. Eventually, after many, many months, it stopped when I realised that there wasn't a solution to be found. The question, 'Am I still a dad?' is still there. The impact of the question is quite different though. I'm not trying to find an answer as much as fill the vacuum that has been left by her death. Find a purpose in life, a reason to keep going. Find a reason to get up each morning and smile because you are doing something that you love. I loved being a dad.

I'd love to find a way to bring the 'daddy-ness' back, have her back. But I can't. Children change our lives in so many ways, ways that we don't appreciate at the time. For me, Evie turned me from being just a man into being a father. The two are definitely not the same thing. One is a fact, the other is a reason for living.

8 May 19

At the end of March, Evie's godfather, David, and I walked the long 13-mile route for Evie's Jurassic 13 (a fundraising walk for Evie's Gift) to see if the route worked, iron out the mapping issues and make sure that we weren't going to scatter bodies over half of Dorset if the route was too tough. During the walk we talked a lot about Evie's Gift and how the work was going. More pointedly, David asked me how I was coping with the workload. Patsy thinks that I am putting too much time into my work – work is tough at the moment, and fundraising in the current climate is particularly hard. Double it up for Evie's Gift and that's where I am. I'm one of those people that thinks, "By the time I have explained what I want done, to this standard and by this time, I could have done it", so I don't ask. But that isn't why I'm working such long hours and find it tough to let go of some of the work.

Granted, I have more invested in Evie's Gift than anyone else, for very obvious reasons. But it is more complex than that. When Evie died, I felt like I had failed her; I had singularly failed to keep her alive. I had one job as a dad and I had messed it up. Highly irrational, I know, because from the first second that the first cell subdivided to become cancer, her fate had been decided. There was nothing that I could ever have done. The position of the tumour made an operation to remove it impossible – a diffuse midline glioma, sat right on top of her brain stem. But that didn't stop me feeling that I had failed as a father. So, in an exhausted state, I took on more and more work in an effort to succeed at something, anything. I needed to prove to myself that I could win, succeed, control things again. I was worn out, so it shouldn't have been a surprise that I struggled enormously to succeed at anything.

But the more I struggled, the more I took on to try and rectify the problem. And so the vicious spiral continued. Our first year at Evie's Gift is over and we need to keep the momentum going to keep the donations flowing, so the pressure continues to mount. I cannot, will not, allow Evie's Gift to fail. And I'm still exhausted, working longer and longer hours. And I still can't step back.

The difference now is that I realise what I have been doing, or trying to do. I recognise that I can't continue at this pace forever. That doesn't mean that I'm slowing down, but it does mean that I'm trying to offload more work on others, especially in fundraising. I reckon I have about two, or maybe three more months at this pace before something gives. Just to add a little more complexity into the mix, we've just had an offer on a new office accepted at work, so I'm adding an office move into the equation. Hey, I was wondering what to do with those unused hours of darkness each day?!

The point of this 'Wednesday Wisdom' isn't about my workload, it is to make the point that as a bereaved parent we have to understand what is going on in our own heads. We have to figure out why we do things in order to learn and change. As if our worlds haven't changed enough. If you know why you are doing something that isn't helpful to your mental health, then you have started helping yourself get through it. You can't do that alone, though. You need true friends to ask some difficult questions and press you for truthful answers. David did that, and so did my counsellor. David and I have known each other for decades and he knows me well enough to speak the truth for my own good. My counsellor doesn't let me hide or ignore the tricky questions. I am very grateful to both of them. Most people avoid asking these questions for fear of upsetting us.

We need someone to hold a mirror up to us and make us look at the image. Sometimes what we see may be all too obvious, or maybe it's tougher to see what the problem is and we need to look a little deeper. But we must do it every now and then. Who can you get to do it for you?

Now the trick is to act on what I have found out. To learn that simply taking on more work won't solve anything, nor will it prove anything, and it certainly won't bring Evie back. It will only make me even more stressed and tired. I need to change something. What that something is will have to be another conversation with David, I suspect.

15 May 19

One of the things that upsets any bereaved parent is to think that their child is being forgotten by those around them. The problem is compounded by two things: firstly, that as time goes by others just get on with their lives, and those moments and anniversaries that are significant to us get missed; secondly, finding ways to keep your child's memory fresh gets harder. We run out of photos to post on Facebook, as we aren't taking new ones, we have the same stories to tell, and finally, people think that we are getting 'better' so they withdraw a little more.

So how can we keep our child's memory alive and fresh? Photo Saturday on the Compassionate Friends closed FB page is a good way of making sure they don't slip away unnoticed, and I do exactly the same thing on my regular Facebook page – for family and friends. It's a chance to see images of Evie that have, until now, been stored away on my laptop. We also sign all cards to people from both of us and EvieAngel. We want our friends to address their cards to us in the same way, or put something like, 'Remembering Evie'.

We've seen some wonderful ways of remembering children – memorial woods where a tree is planted in their name, jewellery made with their fingerprints, benches on their favourite walks. We named a star after Evie in the constellation of Libra, her star sign; tacky I know, but who cares? Finding long-lasting memories is tougher than you might think. I suppose the most permanent and physical way that their name will live on is their headstone. Evie's headstone was fitted a few weeks ago. We wanted something beautiful, unusual, and contemporary. The stones available commercially seemed to be designed for small children, and the adult ones were just too bland for vibrant young woman. We needed something elegant and striking and I hope that we achieved it. I'm not going to post an image here because so many bereaved parents struggle with this decision, and I have no wish to upset them, but am glad to share it privately if you wish to see it. More to the point, go and visit her. We also wanted to avoid clichés and find some words that meant something personal. We chose "I Hope You Dance", words from the Leeann Womack song that we played at her funeral, and a clear message from us to her, and her to us; when times are tough, get up and choose to dance. Carved in Cumbrian slate, we hope that this message will live on forever.

The downside of a headstone is that it is final. When I saw it in place for the first time, the pain slammed into me as I realised that only dead people have headstones; Evie wasn't coming back. But now, a few weeks later, I can look at it as a beautiful way for everyone to see the amazing girl that she was. The girl that we loved more than anything else in the world. We had taken our time to think about what we wanted, sought out an incredible craftsman to give us his ideas, and weren't afraid to change it again and again until we got what we wanted. For us it works, and I truly believe that it will be a long-lasting way of keeping her name alive in the world long after we are gone. #saytheirname

22 May 19

Choice. Losing your child turns your world on its head. It changes you, your relationships, your whole perspective on life. It changes the choices that are available to you as well. Some things are no longer available for you to do. Losing our only child took away so many choices from us. Things to do and share, holidays to go on, guidance that we can't give, places that we can't go or events that we can't be part of. Sitting here now, 15 months after she died, I can't choose to read a book because I was sat in bed reading to her on that horrible last night in the apartment in San Sebastian, before we took her to A&E.

The impact of losing Evie was, and still is, devastating. Friends say, "we don't know how you keep going, I couldn't do it." Our answer has often been, "We don't have a choice, we just get up each day and put one foot in front of the other." But we do have a choice. We could just lay in bed and stay there all day, and in the early days that was very tempting. We 'chose' to get up and start the day.

Choice extends to everything that we do. A year ago, my world was very dark. The analogy that I used was that I was sliding down a steep scree slope, unable to slow down, arms and legs dug into the scree to try and stop the sliding but failing to do so. I felt out of control. And it was at that point that I chose to do something about it. I decided to take some time off and rest and think. I went to the doctor and got some help. I started taking anti-depressants, and I am still taking them. Apparently, there is a stigma about taking them. 'Stigma' is just a word and one I choose to ignore. The pills gave me back the capacity to think, to start a series of other choices that helped me.

I'm now a year on. Evie's death has crystalized and the pain is as heavy now as it ever was. But I also realise now that it is real, final. She won't come back to us. My choices now are different. They are more profound, and far-reaching. In our first year, the choices were short term and fairly straightforward. Now they will affect us and those around us for a long time. Am I going to choose to let Evie's death define me and my future? Am I going to choose to take her with me into the future or am I going to drift? Not long ago, a couple of weeks after the anniversary of Evie's funeral, something changed. I can't say when that was exactly but I made a subconscious decision not to let her death beat me. I spent years telling Evie that she had the talent and strength to do anything that she wanted. All the usual platitudes about the world is your oyster, and all that. So, it's time I stepped up to the plate and practiced what I preached. Don't get me wrong, each and every day the pain is staggering, and to be brutally honest if you told me that I'll go to sleep tonight and wouldn't wake up tomorrow morning, then I wouldn't resist. But I am 'choosing' to fight back against the despair. Finding things that help is hard. I will have a go at anything to see if it works; if it doesn't work, I'll ditch it and try something else.

This decision doesn't belittle what has happened, just the opposite: it reinforces that she was so important to me that losing her has had a world-changing effect on me. But by facing the loss head on, I am recognising that she was, and still is, the most amazing person in the world and that she will make me a better person in a whole new way. I choose to work to preserve her memory and make sure that her name is there forever.

29 May 19

One of the problems that I found after Evie died was that I had, and still have, a whole world of love and nowhere to put it, no-one to give it to. The love of a father for his daughter is completely different. For me, it's all wrapped up in protection, trust, pride, and a connection that is unique in its truest sense. The bond between father and daughter is something special. That's not to downplay the bond between a mother and daughter, or even a father and son, but I believe that the they are all distinctly different. Ask any parent and I think you'll get what I am talking about. Evie always felt safe around me, and I always knew I would protect her to my last breath. To get to her, you would have to go through me.

Evie's death has resulted in feelings of confusion and loss over so many different things. I have a 'need' to be needed, to be the protector, to be the one that this beautiful little girl looks up to for advice, trusting me and my judgement implicitly. You can't buy that feeling, it just evolves with the love between a father and daughter. But now, it's gone. I can't direct that love towards my wife or family, because it isn't the same. What do I do with all this love that has nowhere to go?

We still buy Evie presents and take them to her grave. I talk to her all the time. I say "Morning, Pickle" and "Goodnight, Pickle" every single day. But I've got nowhere to put the love that is still there and is still growing. It's not the sort of thing that you can substitute something else for. A dog would be fabulous but isn't the same. Not only do I not have an answer, I don't even know where to look for one. Is there an answer at all? Does it matter? Is this just another part of the complex set of emotions that we call grief? For a reason that I don't really understand, this is the issue that I find most confusing. I don't like not understanding something and this has me completely baffled. I suppose the simplest way of explaining it is to say that this is what a broken heart feels like.

5 Jun 19

Learn not to care; a strange sentiment. The world that we as bereaved parents inhabit is a weird one. None of the normal rules apply to us, and the 'muggles' out there are mostly oblivious to us and our world. It is an exclusive club that no-one wants to join, and its secrets are masked from everyone until you gain your free membership.

Losing your child is singly the worst thing that can ever happen to any parent. Other problems pale in comparison. Yet if you are like me, the small stuff can take on a magnitude in excess of its true value. I find myself becoming angry at the most trivial event or happening sometimes. Dropping my keys when opening the door, deleting an email by mistake. Add in missing a relative's birthday and things like that, and our world could become completely unmanageable if we let it all get to us. We are already in an emotionally weakened state so we must learn 'not to care'. I have to admit at this point that I'm pretty rubbish at it, but know deep down that I need to learn. Minor things go wrong at work and I need to shrug them off, if only to ease the pressure that I am putting myself under. I know why I am doing it, as I have said in a previous WW, but switching off to work, and what is happening elsewhere while I am on holiday, or at the weekend, is something that I find incredibly hard.

It all comes down to the old adage of looking after yourself. Sometimes, not caring, or at least not giving something 'air time' can be the best thing to do. Focus your energy inwardly, look after yourself, maybe, heaven forbid, even allow yourself to take pleasure in something again. We are so used to caring about our child, about what is happening to them, that we naturally extend that caring attitude to everything else. But now the rules have changed – 'all bets are off'. Like so many bereaved parents, there are times when I feel completely overwhelmed by the mountain of jobs or work that is building up in front of me. But it isn't the volume of work that is the issue. It's my own self-confidence that I'll be able to tackle it. For the first time in a very long time, I didn't work while away on holiday recently. I deliberately ignored the laptop from a work perspective and it felt terrifying. When I got back to work, miraculously the world hadn't stopped going around, Wall Street hadn't crashed, and I got caught up very quickly because I was rested and relaxed. By taking time for myself, and not 'caring' about stuff I was able to heal a little and rest. I was also able to think about Evie a lot because my head wasn't buzzing with the trivia.

There was a small family issue while we were away and I decided not to get involved, because I knew that I'd get sucked in and I wouldn't rest. That was a much harder decision, but one that I had to take for my own sanity. Putting things into perspective is very difficult when all of the boundaries that you once knew have gone, but that's what we have to do. I'm no use to anyone if I'm broken. Bits of me are broken beyond repair, but others can still function if I look after them. And that means being bloody selfish for a bit every now and then.

12 Jun 19

Coping with fatigue has become a constant battle. The fact that grief brings a whole new level of tiredness was thoroughly unexpected, especially as it never seems to abate, not matter what I do to combat it. In the early days, lack of sleep took its toll and that was no surprise, but as time has gone on, you would think that the fatigue would become less of a problem. It hasn't.

The internal white noise, especially last year, when I was trying to find a solution to Evie's death, sucked the energy out of me, but even though I have now managed to unload that drain I am still almost permanently exhausted. Talking to other bereaved parents, it seems that fatigue is a common factor in our lives now and it doesn't ease with time. As I have mentioned before, I have been taking on more and more work in an attempt to prove to myself that I can succeed at something, having 'failed' to keep Evie alive. That has compounded the problem ten-fold. Finally, I managed to start easing off at work, and have now managed to stop myself working at the weekend, offloading some work at Evie's Gift too, but the tiredness remains. I'm sleeping okay in general with the odd bad night, but it doesn't seem to make a difference. I've also been careful about the consumption of alcohol and caffeine, especially in the afternoon and evening.

In a way, I shouldn't be surprised at the fatigue, but it doesn't help with the overall coping mechanism. When you are tired, you don't think straight, or function properly. You can make some fairly dodgy decisions because you haven't thought things through properly. As with all things in our grief-ridden world, we need to recognise the problem before we can tackle it. There seem to be loads of different bits of advice out there on what can help; better diet, exercise, and meditation are a few. As with all things, those that work for me may not work for you, but I am working on the principle that if I try enough of them, something might just come up trumps.

Eating properly and regularly helps, as does exercise, which makes me tired ready for bed. The hassle comes when I wake up early and can't get back to sleep. As soon as I am awake, the realisation that Evie isn't in the next room dawns once again and my brain is off once more. I've been toying with the idea of doing another mindfulness course, as it helped reduce stress some years ago. Our world has enough pain already, so if we can tackle some of the easy things like sleeping better then I reckon that might just have a disproportionate effect and make us feel a lot better.

The major impact though, is from the loss itself and the emotional drain that this has caused. Keeping a mask up for others saps your energy and can only be done for a certain amount of time. Forcing yourself to focus on work or the job in hand takes more, and if you are like me, by mid-afternoon you've run out of steam altogether. I've adapted my work routine to try and cope. I start work early at 6:30 and take short breaks frequently. I snack a lot to keep the carbs flowing, but nothing has yet had a major impact to improve my energy levels. I'm sat here typing away at 8:12 pm and could happily nod off on the sofa. I doubt very much that there's any form of miracle cure here, but I reckon that a combination of diet, exercise, mindfulness, and a recognition that this is the new me will keep my head above the water, at least for a while.

19 Jun 19

Being aware of and, as importantly, understanding what the hell is happening inside your own head, can make an enormous difference to how we all deal with the loss of our children. To me that translated into a level of self-awareness that I had never before got to grips with. Sometimes what I saw wasn't pleasant and I didn't like what I found out. But, self-preservation is vitally important if we are to survive this bitter world of ours.

As usual, I can only write from a personal perspective, and your own experiences could be a world apart from my own. But I figure that one thing is for certain: we all need to understand what is going on in our own heads if we are to make sense of why we do things or why we react the way that we do.

I have always had a vague understanding of my true motives for my actions, but now it has become more of a full-time thing as I battle through the grief and face down the despair. As an example, I knew that I was taking on more and more work in what I thought initially was a desire to just keep busy. Only by stepping back a little and taking an objective look did I come to understand that I was trying to do something completely different; to prove to myself that I could succeed, and overcome the failure to keep Evie alive. Once I understood that, I could formulate a plan to ease out of this self-destructive path. Because it has turned out to be self-destructive. When I wrote a WW a few weeks ago, I thought that I had another two or maybe three months at this pace of work before something broke. I was wrong. I hit the wall almost immediately after writing that piece. I started to recognise symptoms of something more serious, as suddenly I lost the ability to focus and think. If I hadn't been self-aware, I would have ploughed on and imploded. Now, I am more in control and am easing out of the problem in a controlled way.

Initially I saw that as another failure and got angry. But, by holding the mirror up to my anger I have been able to recognise why I was losing my temper so easily and so frequently. Part of it is frustration at myself for not being able to cope with numerous jobs, Evie's death, trying to support Patsy, and a myriad of other minor stuff simultaneously – my car was written off because someone forgot to brake at a roundabout, my mum's roof was leaking, and I'm buying a new office at work, amongst other things. The other part is that it is just a natural progression through the grief 'journey'. All perfectly understandable under these extreme circumstances. Once you've recognised the triggers though, you can take a step back and avoid them.

I had a medical check the other day, as I am approaching 55. My blood pressure was 132/91 which I was pretty chuffed with as it has been nearer 155/95 for the last year. In the good old bad old days, it would have been 115/75 – if I had been any more laid back I'd have been horizontal. So, compared to how high it had been over the last year, I saw it as a marked improvement. The nurse, however, wanted to refer me for further tests as she felt that my 'fight or flight response' was too high – 91 vs the 'normal' maximum of 90! Allowing for the inaccuracies of the kit, I'd have ignored the result. She proceeded to give me a small lecture that I should take more exercise. The red mist started to gather, but because I knew that now was not the time or place to lose my temper, I was able to nod sagely and just say that I had hiked 23 miles the previous weekend, had done 5 miles of hill training carrying 25lbs the night before, and was training to hike 66 miles non-stop in 24 hours carrying about 35lbs on 21st June. I invited her to join my training regime if she thought I needed exercise, but she declined. She still insisted on adding it to my notes. I shrugged my shoulders.

What I have learned, not only from myself, but also by observing others, is that if we understand what we are thinking and why, we can relax a little and not worry about certain things. Before we found The Compassionate Friends for example, we were convinced that we were lost and going through this alone. We aren't. Looking at how others deal with almost identical problems allows you to see what you are doing in a different light and you can look back at your own actions and thoughts, and think "What would I say to someone else in this position who was acting or behaving like that?"

Sometimes we can be our own worst critics, but sometimes we need to be completely honest with ourselves if we are to overcome, or even just live with this massive trauma that we have experienced. The trick for me was to recognise something I didn't like about myself and then just accept it for what it was: an action under extreme stress that was plain okay. The world won't see it that way of course, but you know what? That's okay too. I don't pretend to have it all sorted, far from it. But for some things I am able to rationalise what's happening in my head and know that I can deal with it in a way that won't end in me thumping someone, tempting as it might be.

26 Jun 19

What we do is not always the same as what other people think we are doing. How we are perceived by others, and how our changed world sees them in turn can be confusing for everyone. Including us. But it is also about how we perceive their newly-perceived views of us. Confused yet? Good. Within a very short time following Evie's death my perception of everything around me changed. Death no longer held any fear for me, and I almost welcomed it for myself. Her loss polarised everything; nothing else was important in comparison and to a degree that still holds true. A few weeks ago, my car was written off after someone drove into the back of me at a roundabout, and while I was frustrated at the inconvenience, it didn't really register on the Richter scale of anger. My perception was that it really didn't matter that much.

How we bereaved parents perceive others and their actions is something that the wider world simply doesn't understand. In normal life what you do is one thing, but how your actions are perceived determines the reactions of others. That's just human nature. But for us, our views have changed and we have become hypersensitive to everything. We almost look for problems where none exist. I use the word 'we' in its broadest sense, and I am basing it on my own personal experience. As has been said here before, other people melt away from us and many others change the subject when we want to talk about our dead child. I frequently hear the explanation that people can't cope with it themselves, and that the loss is so alien to them that they would rather avoid it for fear of upsetting us or feeling embarrassed themselves. But. How do they think we then perceive that action? Do they stop and think how their actions make us feel? They imagine that we think, "Oh they can't cope with it so are avoiding the subject because they don't want to hurt us." But that's the excuse they use to justify the action to themselves. I'm afraid that explanation doesn't wash. What we actually think, or perceive, is **"You are demonstrating to me, very clearly, that you think the death of my child is so insignificant as to be unworthy of remembrance**." Our view is that it is an insult to our child, which is why we rage against it. Our perception of an action is significantly different to what the true intention may be. And because their world is so different to our own, they will never know the message that they have just sent. I make no apology for being so direct with this WW. I post my WWs on the Evie's Gift FB page as well, so my family and friends see it. For those that are wonderful, and there are many, I want them to understand why it is so important to me that Evie is remembered and why I will never forgive those that have dishonoured her memory. For those that read it who have melted away, now you know how much your actions hurt, how devastating it is, no matter what your genuine intentions might have been. Life is about action, reaction, and perception. We cannot help how we perceive your actions because our benchmark has changed forever. It is my hope that maybe, just maybe, someone out there, perhaps ex-friends of ours, or friends of other bereaved parents, manage to 'grow a pair' and put aside their short-term discomfort for three minutes and stop and listen to the person whose world has been devastated.

My interpretation of others' actions may well be wrong, or too extreme, but the trauma that any bereaved parent goes through changes everything in their world to such a degree that is beyond comprehension for those that are outside it. We are battered and bruised beyond belief and that means that our perception of what is happening to us is changed forever. With our damaged perception there is a risk that we will hunker down and withdraw, and that sends out a message to others that they perceive as isolationist, rather than us simply trying to protect ourselves from yet more pain. Dragging the concept of perception out into public view might just open a few eyes to our pain. But we have to look inward for a little while and understand how we are perceiving others and their actions too. Are we inadvertently contributing to the problem in some way? Are we being honest with our friends? We must learn to recognise what we are doing and why. It's not a situation where we can find a compromise position, but one of understanding and recognition. It isn't right or wrong, it is just what our new world looks like.

3 July 2019

Ten days ago, Pats and I went to a memorial service in Bristol, organised by the Bristol Royal Hospital for

Children for parents who had lost a child that had been treated there. We caught up with some of the staff that had been there during our month-long stay, and met up again with other parents that had been there at the same time. But that isn't what this WW is about. What became apparent very quickly was the huge gap between what non-bereaved people think we want and what us bereaved parents actually want, or even need. Don't get me wrong, in the main the event was fine, it was well-organised and was held in a lovely venue, but what stood out was that even though it was the bereavement team who had pulled it together, they had little real concept of what bereavement as a parent is all about.

A humanist celebrant talked briefly about loss – but very quickly this supposedly sensitive person trotted out practically every cliché and platitude that we all hate. It was the most patronising piece I have had to listen to since Evie died. We could have played 'Platitude Bingo'. I sat there open-mouthed as she spouted one after another. "Your child wouldn't want you to be sad", "They've gone to a better place", "Look after yourself", "Take joy in the small things." The next guy stood up and said "What a privilege is was to be there", as if we were a bunch of VIPs. Trite nonsense. For the majority of the performance, 60-odd parents sat there in stunned silence.

We were invited to join in singing 'happy' songs like 'Over the Rainbow', presumably designed to cheer us all up. Conversely, all the presenters were very solemn and spoke very softly, as if we would break down if they spoke any louder. Evie's funeral had more laughs.

To offer some form of balance, there were lovely moments too – a short piece read from four different faiths, and we were invited to place a star with our children's name on it on a memory wall. A final poem on the order of service, that unfortunately wasn't read out, was lovely. But overall, it served to demonstrate for me the huge gap between us and the rest of the world. And this was a hospital's specialist bereavement team! If they can get it so spectacularly wrong, what chance has the rest of the world got? We were invited to complete a feedback questionnaire. I've been polite, but forthright, and recommended that next time they get in touch with The Compassionate Friends to see how it should be done. As with so many things in our new world, it was done with the best of intentions, but with no real concept of what was needed. Rant over.

10 Jul 19

Do bereaved parents suffer from survivor's guilt? I know that I would gladly change places with Evie, and have struggled to figure out why I am still here and Evie isn't. Losing a child is certainly a major trauma, and it strikes me that it is intrinsically wrong for any parent to outlive their child. The death of our child has also released feelings that I could have done more to keep her alive. I say 'feelings', because fundamentally I know beyond any doubt that nothing that we could have done would have changed the outcome in any meaningful way. Her death is certainly affecting my ability to function normally. Pull those facts together and you have the classic symptoms of survivor's guilt.

I'm not sure that I recognise what I'm feeling as 'guilt', as such, but I most definitely would give anything to have Evie back. I would swap anyone for her; me, Patsy, anyone. I know for a fact that losing Evie makes me feel that I no longer have a purpose in life, when, had she and I swapped places, she would have a life to lead, a contribution to make. I know that we did everything that could be done to make her last few weeks as comfortable as possible, as well as fighting to get the surgeons in Bristol to carry out the final de-bulking operation to remove more of the tumour, which would buy us more time with her. The rational part of my brain is utterly convinced that we made the right decisions at every stage of her illness. The emotional side, though, struggles to deal with the outcome and questions why she had to be taken from us.

It might be more accurate to call it 'survivor questioning'. I keep asking myself so many questions, but rarely get beyond the question itself. I keep going around in circles, repeating the question over and over, never actually managing to start answering it. I watch the news every day and see items on some terrorist or thug beating up an older person, and my reaction is always the same – how come this piece of scum gets to live, when our child, with so much to give, has been taken? It would be nice to get an answer to the questions so that I can get some peace. Another topic for the counsellor, I guess?

As with all things, understanding the 'why', means that we can start tackling the 'how'. I have a feeling that this one is going to take a long time to sort out.

17 Jul 19

I have talked briefly about anti-depressants and stress before, usually as a passing shot within another subject, but I've not really got to grips with the whole topic in isolation. Losing a child is without doubt **the** worst thing that can happen to a parent, and the impact is enormous. Part of you dies with your child, and PTSD undoubtedly rears its ugly head.

I have been taking anti-depressants for over a year now and the dosage has increased in that time. Our culture definitely stigmatises them, but they get me through the day: they allow me to function and think. Without them, I would be in a very different place. I take my hat off to those of you that keep going without them because I don't know that I'm up to it. I am not ashamed in the least that I need them to survive. The word 'need' is important here. I know that I most definitely do not want to be the little old man that everybody pities, but I also know that I'm not finished here on this earth and have yet to find the ultimate way to maintain Evie's memory. To do that I have to be able to think clearly and plan. It's unfinished business. I need the pills to help me do that.

I have had conversations with friends about the pills, and when they mention the word 'depression', or 'anti-depressants' they do so in hushed tones. Why? Are they worried that someone out there will overhear the conversation and judge me? I don't care. Let's be very clear, my beautiful child is dead and that has made me suffer from depression. I take pills to counteract the effects of that depression and am still pretty much stressed to my eyebrows most days. I am not ashamed that I need pills to get me through the day. I would be positively worried if I thought that how the world looked at me was more important than surviving the most devastating thing that I can experience. I am a 55-year-old man, who flew a multi-million aeroplane for the RAF taking troops around the globe, led the first Hercules 3-ship formation into Kosovo ahead of the Russians, completed two tours of duty in the Falkland Islands, and yet losing Evie has broken me. Not hurt, broken. I freely admit that I am not strong enough to work through this without chemical help.

As the song says, 'I am what I am'. If anyone out there thinks that taking anti-depressants is a sign of weakness, then you go for it, mate, because until you have walked a yard, let alone a mile in my shoes, you will have no concept of what this feels like. We must find the help, the strength, the willpower to survive wherever we can, and if a few pills can do that then that's just fine by me.

When will I start to wean myself off them? No idea. Originally, I had hoped that it might be six months or maybe a year. But that has changed. I'll do it when I'm ready, when I feel that I am getting to grips with the pain, and not before. When I won't unravel without them. The stigma sits with those who may wish to judge me and no-one else. So, in the best tradition of Alcoholics Anonymous, "**Hello, my name is Bryan, I am suffering from depression and I take anti-depressants**."

24 Jul 19

Sometimes a word or phrase can come into sharp focus, even though you've heard it many times before. I was washing up the other morning with the radio on and the song 'This is Me' from *The Greatest Showman* was playing. It struck me, while actually listening to the words for once, that it resonates with the world that I now live in, and the person that I am, the person that I have become.

I've said before in previous WWs that we change following the death of our children, that we will never be the same again. But the message that I was trying to get across then was that others need to accept who we are. Listening to that song, I realised that **I** need to accept who I am, who I have become. I have never tried to go back to the old me, but I don't want to accept the new one either. 'Caught between a rock and a hard place' is the phrase that best describes it. Looking deeper, it isn't that I don't like the person that I have become, although there are definitely aspects that I need to tackle, it is more about I don't like 'why' I have become this person. If Evie were still here, I wouldn't be displaying these new character traits.

I have always been a realist, in the truest sense of the word, and I think I still am. So, it should be relatively simple to rationalise the problem, figure out that this change is permanent as Evie won't magically pop back into my life, and accept it for what it is. So why can't I do that? Because to do so also means that I have to accept that I can't bring her back. By fighting the 'new me' I am trying to hang on to my old life with Evie in it. It's all part of the whole 'acceptance' bit of the grief journey, but it has a permanence that you can't avoid. We battle away against the inevitable in the hope that something will change. Perhaps hope gives us the strength to face the continual pain until we are ready to accept the truth? Perhaps hope gives us something positive to look at amongst the despair? Perhaps hope is simply what keeps us going through those lonely mornings and dark nights lying awake?

The new me is more volatile than before. I lose my temper faster. Some people struggle to accept who I have become following Evie's death. Single words or images can trigger an emotional fall that can be rapid and painful to witness. I recover quickly in the main, but it still hurts. I distinctly remember listening to 'This is Me' driving back from hospital one evening in the winter of 2017 thinking then that it could so easily be applied to Evie, her self-belief, her strength. Now it can be applied just as easily to me, but for a different reason. I'm cherry-picking from the lyrics a bit, but the words of the song are still there to be listened to. Like the song says, I make no apologies for who I am, this is me.

The drum that I am now marching to is the one that wants to preserve Evie's name and memory and love those closest to me. This is me. To those out there that find talking to a bereaved parent difficult, accept it or 'move on'. For myself, this is the new 'me' so I have to learn to live with it.

31 Jul 19

As part of the support that we still receive from Julia's House Hospice, we each see one of the nurses that looked after Evie about once every 4-6 weeks. Last month I met Lisa in a coffee shop in Devizes and we chatted about how I was feeling, the struggles I was having around Father's Day and my birthday. It isn't counselling as such, just an hour chatting through what has been going on. We were joined at the end by Dawn, an Evie's Gift trustee, who was collecting some merchandise from me to sell at a summer fete. Lisa was talking about a new programme that JHH want to set up, bringing together bereaved parents to support each other locally, and she wanted my thoughts. My normal reaction would have been to volunteer to help run it, but right now I'm drowning in work anyway and am far too tired. Dawn's comment was pretty straightforward:

"You don't want Bryan doing it as he'll try and 'fix' everyone." Or words to that effect.

Two weeks later we were at a support group meeting and one of the other bereaved parents was talking about work and I threw in my two pennies' worth. This time is was my wife who told me to stop trying to 'fix' the problem. At the time I felt a little aggrieved, but on reflection she was right. They were both right. My natural reaction now is to try and fix peoples' problems. I don't stop and think, I just get on with it. Why do I do that? What am I trying to achieve? Did I do that before Evie was ill?

Looking back pre-illness, I had tried to help out where I could, but it was always tempered by reality. If I wasn't able to commit the time to something then I stood back. But now I don't, I pile in whenever and wherever the opportunity presents itself. The reason is simple enough – I couldn't 'fix' Evie so I'm trying to compensate by fixing other people instead. Not a massive revelation really, but an important point for me. It points to an unresolved issue in my head around caring for someone that I love. As time progresses, the mental issues that I face are distilling into two or three core problems. Ones that are rooted deep and will require time and effort to unpick. I had a conversation with Patsy after a counselling session as I had been talking about why I still find it hard to unload work. Her view was that I wasn't getting value from the sessions as we went over the same ground time and again. I have a different take on it; the problem is too important to gloss over and needs the time and attention to work through it. There's another point too. These two or three issues impact on many different areas of my life and in different ways, and manifest themselves in all sorts of different behaviours.

The more I try and figure out what is happening in my head, the more I discover that everything is interrelated and the ripples from one problem touch another. My life feels like a giant ball of Christmas lights in a huge tangle with some blown bulbs, some flashing intermittently, and others missing altogether. There are days when I just can't be bothered to try and untangle part of it, and others when I attack it with gusto. Sorry for very thoroughly mixing my metaphors, but that in itself is an accurate representation of my world. I'm a mixed metaphor!

I suppose what I am trying to say, in a rather long-winded way, is that there is no quick 'fix' for me.

7 Aug 19

You have my permission to step on the eggshells. As my feelings about losing Evie have evolved, I have come to realise that in the main, some people genuinely want to help, but simply don't know how. They have a great fear of upsetting me by saying the wrong thing, or reminding me that Evie has died, and therefore causing me pain. Some just feel lost about what to say at all. I don't need 'reminding' about her death; I will never forget. Talking about her is wonderful, and any conversation that includes her, especially those instigated by someone else, are a gift. I think that sometimes, as a bereaved parent, I am at risk of becoming insular, and that in itself creates an atmosphere of fear amongst my friends, which is exactly what I don't want to do. People walk on eggshells because of their uncertainty over what to say. Sadly, some just don't give a shit about anyone else, and I'm better off without them in my life.

So … You have my permission to walk on the eggshells, crush them underfoot, sweep the remnants away. Talk freely about Evie in any way that you feel, but at least talk, say something. I am convinced now that it is up to me to set the standard, to show that you cannot hurt me any more than I am already hurt. That by ignoring her you are indeed causing pain, intentionally or otherwise. It is too easy for me to look at everyone else and blame them for not caring. I need to take control, to guide and lead, to challenge you, to let everyone know that saying nothing isn't acceptable. To tell you that if you say something that I find hard to hear, or is upsetting, then that's fine and I'll live with it. If I need a moment, then I'll take a moment, and we can pick up where we left off.

In the same way, although we are the ones that are in pain and need friendship, it is also up to us to seek that friendship out. If you invite me out for a coffee, and I turn you down because I'm having a bad day, then keep asking. Or maybe I will take the lead and do the asking? I can sit in the corner hurting, or control my own destiny. I shouldn't have to but I will, because if I don't, if other bereaved parents don't, then there is a risk that we will become little hermits in a world that is getting on with its life. We are giving the people that we moan about the excuse that they are looking for to stay away. Social isolation is crippling, but we can do something about it if we choose to. Friendship is a two-way street. So, let's take control again and force them to face their own mini-demons. If they choose to stay away, then we will know that we have at least tried, as hard as that may have been.

This isn't a 'Get Out of Jail Free' card to my friends who have chosen to keep their distance, it is me telling you, very clearly, that if the reason that you have stayed away is from fear of not knowing what to say, then that doesn't matter: just say something about Evie. This Christmas, if you don't mention Evie in your card in some way, then that will be the cruellest blow. Last year, every card that didn't mention her went straight in the bin.

Losing a child isn't contagious, I promise. If you still can't manage to support a friend whose life has been devastated beyond belief, then my recommendation is that you take a long hard look in the mirror and examine what is staring back at you. If I can look deep into my soul, having faced the most painful event in my life, then you with your 'normal' family life, your kids playing near you, shouldn't have any problems. Unless of course, you don't actually give a shit after all? Just hit 'Like' and make some comment about how nice the picture of Evie is. I know, sarcasm is the lowest form of wit, and the last resort of the small-minded, but it works.

11 Aug 19

I guess this is more of a 'Law of Unintended Consequences' kind of piece. One of the things that I have come to appreciate from my closest friends is that they are honest with me all the time, even when it might be difficult for them to broach a subject. David – one of Evie's godfathers – and I were talking on the phone this morning and we got chatting about my book and the Wednesday Wisdoms. David asked me who I was aiming these pieces at and, as I post them on the Evie's Gift FB page too, had I thought about how they were interpreted by those that read them. His view, I think, was that what I write is from the heart, is raw, and can be difficult reading, that I might in some way actually be creating eggshells rather than sweeping them away. Because he and I have been friends for decades, I took it as a comment, not a criticism; he cares enough to raise it.

So, on the basis of that conversation, just for the Evie's Gift FB friends, this is what the WWs are all about and what I am aiming to achieve from them. It'll also go on The Compassionate Friends page because it might shed some light there too.

I write from the heart. What I feel is utterly, brutally honest, always. They are still written primarily with TCF bereaved parents as their target audience. I have posted them on the Evie's Gift page because it seems to me that what Pats and I are going through is so alien to that group, that if our friends understand what we feel and why they may just get a taste of what this alien world is like. If you know why someone is behaving the way they are, then it goes some way to help you deal with them. For our closest, truest, and most wonderful friends, if you read them and think that you may have done something 'wrong' or inadvertently hurt us, it's okay. Because we see you frequently, we will tell you loud and clear if there's something we don't like or if it hurts. There are many other people that I would like to read the WWs to understand what I am saying and why. Some of the content might make some people feel a little uncomfortable. If it does, then the solution is straightforward. Talk to me. Ask.

The most recent WW talked about eggshells. I wrote it to express an ongoing frustration that I feel, and aimed it mostly at people who are at a distance but don't want to be. They are the people in the middle ground, not knowing what to do. I suppose it was a cry for help, intermingled with my continuing anger at losing Evie. I had thought about writing that particular piece from three different perspectives but it would have been huge. So, I stuck with plan A. One of the things that I talk about in the book is how I lose my temper frequently, and how minor frustrations get bent out of shape. I lash out and whoever happens to be in range gets it between the eyes. Sometimes, that extends to my writing too – I am most definitely in the angry phase of my grief journey so sometimes it bubbles to the surface, in case you hadn't noticed. An unintended consequence. One of the by-products of grief is that your social filters get turned off. Our society isn't used to honesty and it can be a shock when confronted by it.

It's interesting to look at the comments on the two pages, The Compassionate Friends and Evie's Gift, and compare them. When a piece is hard-hitting or painful, the EG page comments drop away but the TCF ones don't, because the level of understanding amongst other bereaved parents is higher. They get it because they are experiencing it too. In the last WW I deliberately made a statement at the end to see who actually read them and who didn't. Harsh? Yep. But as we work our way through this painful world, I need to know who I can rely on and who will be there when I need them. Self-preservation is extremely important.

Will I change my style? I doubt it. Am I more aware of the collateral damage? Yes, thanks to the honesty and true friendship of someone I would trust with my life. If fact, I had trusted him with Evie's life, as he was her nominated guardian should anything have happened to Patsy and I. And that, people, is what I have been banging on about all this time. Friendship, honesty, and love. It's all a bereaved parent needs.

14 Aug 19

In Bath last summer we had the 'Owl Trail' – 83 painted or decorated owls, all about 1.1m high painted by local artists and forming a trail around the city and local area. The idea was that you visited them all to 'collect' them, answer questions to gain points, and win a prize. Evie used to enjoy doing these trails so we decided to have a go. We found all 83 and decided that when they came up for auction in the charity fundraiser we would try and buy one, as there were a few that had particular resonance for us. Long story short, we managed to buy an owl called Glimfeather, painted by local artist Laura Fearn; it had been displayed in Waterstones and was covered in small quotes from children's stories. It was perfect because Evie loved reading. Then, to my utter amazement, at the end of the auction we won the raffle, which was a blank owl!

We asked Laura to decorate the blank owl with images of Evie's favourite cuddly toys and an image of Evie reading a book, and decided to donate it to the Royal United Hospital in Bath as their oncology team had looked after Evie when she was at home. We named it EvieOwl, and her name is painted onto her talons. Last Thursday we visited the hospital to see the place in the Brownsword Therapy Centre where it will be displayed for everyone to see. And it was here that I suddenly realised that I didn't want it to go; I had formed some kind of attachment to it. Part of me wanted to give them Glimfeather instead. Having two dirty great owls in the lounge is daft, so one of them has to go. But why have I formed such as attachment to this one? It wasn't Evie's, it wasn't something that she had wanted or talked about. It was new and we had designed it deliberately for this purpose, to go to the hospital to get Evie's name out there and for others to enjoy. So why did I feel so attached to it? It will definitely go to the hospital for display there, but it opened up thoughts around attachment to Evie's things, or things associated with her.

We've talked about Evie's possessions at The Compassionate Friends Support Group and at bereavement retreats. We have kept almost all of her stuff with only things that she had outgrown given to others or sold. That said, the loft is full of her Sylvanian Families toys and Thomas the Tank Engine trains and track as we can't part with them. It is another classic example of an illogical approach. It's just 'stuff'. Most of it has no emotional attachment. We have jewellery we had bought for her for when she was older, but can't bring ourselves to give it away. We have her saxophone, which her junior school could make good use of, yet we find it so hard to hand it over.

Her books and teddies are simple to rationalise, especially as some of them smell of her. But the other things that she no longer liked or played with? Why can't we move them on? Who knows? I guess the point is that it doesn't matter. We'll make a decision one way or another when we are ready.

Evie Owl will be at her new home very shortly, and when the Therapy Centre opens in September hundreds of people will be able to enjoy her, and Evie's name will be seen by them. But I will miss her terribly.

21 Aug 19

Being a bereaved parent isn't a badge that you can wear, so that everyone knows. We aren't a minority group expecting, or demanding equal rights. We haven't been trampled underfoot. We just want a bit of normality now and again. Some understanding. And I think that we can expect friends to understand who we have become and how we hope to be treated, to help us along with our healing. But you know what? We too have to remember that the world goes on around us, time ticks over and that is to be expected. Everyone else's lives will continue.

One of the things that was pointed out recently is that people around us not only worry about upsetting us by talking about Evie, but also don't want to talk about their own lives and their own issues because compared to our pain, it isn't as 'big'. When this was mentioned to me, I was quite surprised that this was the way people thought, that they don't mention their own tribulations because we might feel that they are insignificant in some way. To me this reinforces the point that we are in charge of our own destiny and can influence how people behave around us. To talk about a sick cat, about a cruddy boss at work, or the struggle that someone else may be having with cancer is an important part of life for our friends, so it must be an important part of our lives too. Friendship is a two-way street, and we are quite possibly uniquely placed to help.

One of the essential parts of the healing process for any person who has undergone a major trauma is helping others. For a bereaved parent, being able to help a friend or family member is an opportunity to find value in yourself once again: a purpose. I can't speak for everyone else of course, but for me, being able to listen to someone else's issues and offer a thought or advice is a way to feel involved again, to be part of life once more. So, from a personal perspective, don't hold back, don't not (nice double negative there!) talk about your granny who has cancer just because it might be a tough conversation for me. I might just have that unique insight into what is happening and might just be able to help. I'm more resilient than you might think. Christ, my daughter died and I'm still standing, so nothing that you can throw at me is going to phase me. At my age, most of my friends have lost parents and are hurting too with their own pain. For them, this is the worst thing that they have experienced. I can be a friend too. I can take the load for a while if you need me to. I can listen to you, just as easily as you can listen to me.

As I have said in these WWs so many times, the world of a bereaved parent is so complex that there is no guide book, so we all kind of make it up as we go along. Both us and our friends. I want, no I need, to feel valued, so asking for my input makes me feel part of the community again, and you get a different view. I won't judge your problem, or score it on a scale of 1 to 10 compared to losing Evie. It is most certainly not one of those, 'my dad is bigger than your dad' things. Sure, I might find the subject matter difficult, but so what? At least you are talking to me, and if I can help I will.

28 Aug 19

Self-Doubt. I may have touched on this subject previously, so if you've heard it all before, I apologise. While my self-doubt isn't as bad this year as it was last, it is most definitely still there. I have been procrastinating over a number of issues recently, and while part of that problem can be put down to the lack of energy and motivation to tackle the tricky problems, there's no such excuse for the easy ones. It's a fear of failing, pure and simple. I doubt my ability to make a sensible decision. Tracking it back, I can see clearly that it is part and parcel of the whole 'failing to keep Evie alive' problem. If I don't make a decision, I can't get it wrong.

But what I am finding difficult to understand is that at the same time, I am desperately still looking for successes to demonstrate to myself that I have value and can still make a contribution. Total contradiction. You'd think that one or the other would dominate but it doesn't happen that way. I want to make a decision, but can't because I don't trust my own judgement any more. I look to others for validation, not quite to take the decision away, but to give an opinion or view that supports my own, to prove to myself that I'm right. I think in some way, because of the self-doubt, I may have set the bar too high. I may be expecting too much of myself all the time. I know that I can't be 100% right 100% of the time, but I have a feeling that is what I am aiming for. Procrastination is worse than making a wrong decision in my view. It's not 'me'; it's not the old 'me'. The trouble is, that the procrastination adds to the self-doubt because it shows that I can't even make a decision about making a decision, let alone get it right.

The second year without Evie has been very different from the first and my emotions have changed dramatically. The rawness of the loss is still there but other issues have now become obvious. Anger for one. Oh my God, am I angry. Self-doubt is another. There is no logic for the self-doubt. I know, absolutely categorically that if given my time again with Evie's illness that I would make exactly the same decisions, make the same choices on treatment and still bring her home for those last precious six weeks. I know, deep in my soul, that every single decision that Patsy and I took on Evie's treatment was right. Each decision was the right one at the right time. We always placed Evie's needs first, we were always motivated by one thing and one thing only – Evie's life had to be as pain-free and comfortable as possible. Nothing else intervened, ever. Even with 20/20 hindsight I wouldn't change any of those major decisions. So why the self-doubt now? I have proven to myself and everyone else that beyond any doubt that our decisions were spot on, so why do I doubt my decision-making capabilities now? Faced with agonising decisions, under enormous pressure we got it right. If I can do it under such terrible pressure, why can't I do it now?

Is there something deeper that I am troubled by? Is it a natural part of grieving? Because of who I am, I have to know. I have to understand what is happening because, put simply, I don't like it. By not making decisions, I am pushing work down the path and building up a bow wave of work which just makes me feel overwhelmed. I need to get to the bottom of this one. Standby by for "Self-Doubt: The Sequel". Maybe.

4 Sep 19

My very first WW was about being kind to yourself. I said at the time that I didn't have a clue what that actually meant. Six months down the line from that first scribbling, I think I'm getting to grips with the concept. As with everything else that Patsy and I have had to face along the way, it isn't simple, and impacts on so many different areas of our lives, and it in turn is impacted by other things. I'm almost back to the tangled Christmas lights analogy!

I think being kind to yourself is far more important than I first realised and actually, should be more accurately represented as 'self-preservation'. The trials that we face as bereaved parents are far greater than most people realise and, therefore, need greater effort to tackle. Forgive yourself for the mistakes, the bad tempers, the inward-looking days that you have. Don't get upset with yourself if you can't cope. You may feel indebted to family or your work, but you know what? If you don't cut yourself some slack every now and then, life will become intolerable. These are the easy things though. The trickier part is standing up for yourself, making everyone else understand what is happening, taking control (a previous WW) of how friends and colleagues treat you.

Work is an important part of our lives for so many reasons. It pays the bills, but also gives you something else to think about, easing out of the pain for a little while. This is why a safe work environment is crucial. If work isn't somewhere that you can go and feel cared about then you need to have a long hard think about it. Unless you work for someone that has lost a child, the management team aren't going to understand properly, but decent employers will want to care for their staff because they recognise that you will repay that patience and trust with loyalty. Too often though, work can become a place of stress. Our capabilities as work-mates are weakened through the death of our child. We make unforced errors and struggle when the pressure increases; our minds are dominated by the child's death. A good employer will cut you some slack, talk to you openly and honestly about how you can work together to the benefit of both you and the business.

But … some employers are either too ill-informed or too selfish to bother; too greedy to care. The focus is on one thing only – their bank balance. Your needs come second, third, or even at the bottom of the pile. This is the point where you need to think about what is best for you. Maybe work fewer days, or change roles within the organisation, or even look elsewhere. It's a tough decision to take and has all sorts of risks associated with it, but you are worth more, deserve better and the best way to preserve what sanity you have left as a bereaved parent is to be kind to yourself and put yourself and your health first. Looking after yourself should be top of the tree; work should be a place where you can go and free your mind of the pain for a little while each day.

Being kind to yourself, looking after yourself, sometimes means doing something radical. Maybe being kind to yourself evolves with time as you gain strength into 'stand up for yourself'? Don't let others get away with treating you badly.

11 Sep 19

Finding some sort of outlet for the grief is an important part of healing for me. After Evie died and her book was published, I started to think about writing something myself, although I had no idea what. These Wednesday Wisdoms were the first piece of writing. Evie loved writing. For her it was stories, fiction. For me it was something else. It was unloading the pain. These Wednesday Wisdoms became an outlet, a way of tackling those horrible thoughts that had dogged my brain, and doing so publicly meant that I couldn't ignore them. The mere act of writing makes me think more deeply about a problem, or a thought. It means that, as I am going to 'publish' it, I have to be honest. I can't hide from it because I'll get found out. If it is in the public domain, then I have to tackle it head on. The act of writing has not only been cathartic, it has helped me to face those difficult issues that I might otherwise have hidden from. One part of the journey leads inexorably to the next, and the next, and the next.

By putting the pain down on paper, it has also been a way of expressing the pain, approaching it in a way that I can come back to again and again over time, to think it through. It is an outlet for me because I can express whatever I want, however I want. I can write and think about all sorts of things. The pain that runs through me every single day has an exit point. It can flow freely. It can escape because the writing is honest. Evie was honest, so I have to be.

Losing Evie was devastating. It is a level of pain so excruciating that it is impossible to comprehend if you haven't been there. It demands an escape route or simply corrodes you from the inside. Finding a way of releasing the pressure is vital for me, otherwise I would implode. For some it might be work, or exercise. For me it has turned out to be writing. It's a cliché that these traumatic emotions can build like a pressure cooker, but they do. They need to escape. So, it's true.

I have learned over the last six months that the writing can't be forced. It flows when it flows. It's not one of those 'I'll sit down between eight and nine o'clock and write' kind of things. When an idea or thought strikes, I stop what I'm doing and write. I have to let the thoughts flow in whatever order they come, which is why some of the Wednesday Wisdoms are a bit disjointed; the book is certainly disjointed. There are inconsistencies, repetitions and contradictions. But that doesn't matter, because the whole point is that the pain is released, and if it is out there then it can't hide any more. Whatever form your outlet takes is yours to own. If it works for you then that's fine.

For me, I'll keep writing, either privately or publicly. I might start a second book, or I might not. I might keep writing Wednesday Wisdoms or I might not. I might find another form of writing. But I will write. It's my only outlet and I need it.

18 Sep 19

We all have bad days. We always have done. Those days where nothing seems to go right for some unknown reason. Now though, they seem to come more frequently and can develop into bad weeks or bad months. The problem that I have found is that a 'normal' bad day, when things just don't come together, or when you get a series of frustrations, are magnified by the loss of our child. Where before I would have come home, had a general grumble and a glass of wine and forgotten about it, I now sit and stew or get sucked into it. We are pulled in even by the minor irritations. They can get blown out of all proportion.

The other day I experienced a series of very minor problems, all of which were pretty trivial but collectively, when added to the background pain, became a torrent that I felt I couldn't fight off. I felt battered by it all. It took an enormous amount of willpower to step back, take an objective look, and then start to tackle them one at a time. Within an hour or so, I had sorted most of them out and things were back to 'normal' again. I just wrote a list and worked my way through it. But it would have been very easy to let the tide of negativity overwhelm me, to just let it all become too much. There are times when life just feels like I am wading through treacle up to my neck. What were once minor irritations have become something more problematic, not because of what they are, but because of where I am. Because of my ability to cope, or not cope.

To get through these bad days, I need something to hang on to, something to fight for, to make life worth living. By harnessing that energy, I can then put the body armour on and face down the problems. Strangely, the big issues are easier. I seem to find energy from somewhere, focus, and deal with them. Not sure why that happens, but it does.

But it's all exhausting. Tackling even the minor stuff takes energy. I've learned over time to pace myself (yeah right, I hear Patsy say!), and that I will be exhausted far more quickly than before. This means that I have to stop when the time comes and not worry about what might be left over; it can wait for another day. My new routine recognises that I am at my most productive first thing in the morning and that I gradually fade as the day progresses until, by mid-afternoon, I've lost all willpower and energy to do very much. I stop for an hour or so at that point and do something mindless: watch a DVD, cut corks in half for the bird boxes I am making, or just read the paper. Whatever takes my fancy. When I am ready, I start again and pick up where I left off. Unless something is vital, it can be done tomorrow.

For me, self-awareness is the vital part of the 'issue' equation. I know how I am going to feel or be, so I know what I need to do to sort it out. I have also learned to recognise when I am most likely to be at a low ebb, so can prepare for it. Next week is Evie's birthday, and the last week or so has been pretty low. Actually, that's not truthful; they've been horrible. The next 6 days are going to get steadily worse until her birthday on 24 September, but I know it is coming. I know how I am going to feel, so I am ready for it, unlike last year when it came as a shock. I'm not sure yet how I am going to face it, but I know I will because I've done it before and survived.

25 Sep 19

Yesterday should have been Evie's 15th birthday, instead she is forever 13. It was a tough day, but I think that it is now time to tackle the elephant in the room, both for bereaved parents like myself, and also for friends and family who may well be living in 'the dark' or quite possibly 'in denial'. This WW comes with a health warning: it's going to tackle a taboo subject, a very delicate subject; suicidal feelings. Please be clear, it isn't a cry for help. It is my, probably very clumsy, attempt to make a wider audience aware of how this world of ours **really** feels: you must look beyond the smiling face that you may see. I have tried to keep the language in this WW moderate.

Evie's death (not 'passing') ripped a hole in our lives that can never be filled. We created Evie out of nothing and when she died, we lost a part of ourselves, we lost our future and our reason to be here. That last part is the elephant: our reason to be here. Without Evie, what's the point? Everything that we did was for Evie. Our work, our plans, our lives, were all there to prepare her for adulthood. That has gone. So why bother carrying on? It's a subject that never gets discussed. It is hidden from view, but that doesn't mean it isn't there. For many, out of sight quite literally means out of mind. It cannot stay that way. Like so many mental health issues, it must be out in the open so that it can be tackled.

Shortly after Evie died, I mentioned to our doctor that I had been experiencing constant headaches for many weeks. When you think about the stress that I had been under for the previous three months, that isn't a great surprise, but as Evie had died from a brain tumour, he wasn't taking any chances, so he sent me for a CT scan the next day and asked them to expedite the result. He rang me that very evening and said that everything was clear and I was fine. I was disappointed. All I wanted was to be with Evie again. Twenty months on, I still feel like that. There are various bits and pieces of me that are breaking, some more seriously than others, all part of getting older most likely. If one turned out to be very serious, I think I'd actually feel relief. The grief would be finite at last.

The face that we bereaved parents present to the world is often governed by how others wish to view us. We hear time and again that we are 'strong', 'amazing', or 'inspiring'. We're none of those things. We just don't have a choice. At some time or other in our grief journey, I think it is safe to say that the vast majority of bereaved parents just want the pain to be over and want to be with their children again. I'm no different. I have spent a lot of time trying to rationalise it, but the grief stops you from doing that because it is too powerful. I don't know what Evie would want me to do because I can't ask her. "Evie would want you to carry on," is nothing more than a meaningless platitude. I can presume that she might be pissed off that, when her life had been taken from her, I threw mine away. If I'm not here, I can't honour her memory.

As I have said before, I take anti-depressants to help me through the day. That dosage doubled a few months ago and last week it doubled again. And for me, that 'why bother' question came back. Evie died 20 months ago, and in that time the temptation to join her has been strong on four occasions. Each time I have literally, as well as figuratively, stepped back. Yet, people tell me that I am strong or inspiring. I think you can see from those few lines above that I don't feel strong. The pills help to control the chemical reactions in my brain and help me to regain some capacity for rational thought. When you add this to open and honest (honest with myself!) talks with my counsellor, then it gives you the tools to continue. But the pain never ever goes away, and it is a constant, exhausting battle to get through each day. It grinds you down.

For bereaved parents who may be reading this, you aren't alone, you aren't going mad, we all have those moments of despair. Sometimes, those moments are there for a while, but they can be worked through with friendship, strength, and determination. There will continue to be times when it is all just too much to cope with, and for those times we need our closest friends. And that is to be expected. When those friends can't cope themselves, then there is The Compassionate Friends, the wonderful group that shares our pain and understands in a way that is impossible for everyone else.

For the friends and family reading this, look beyond the smile, the façade, the bravado. Underneath is a soul in turmoil that needs to be loved and cared about. If you think I'm 'strong', I'm not. I'm broken, utterly broken. But now the elephant is out there for all to see, and it's time to go big game hunting.

EPILOGUE

As I said right at the beginning, this isn't a survival guide, just a series of thoughts and feelings from a man who has pretty much lost his purpose in life and spent a long time floundering. Evie's death broke me. Completely. It took me to a place that was terrifying. If you are a bereaved parent, then I genuinely hope that you have drawn something from it, whatever that might be. If you are a 'muggle', a non-bereaved parent, then I hope that you now have a slightly better understanding of what it feels like to have your life ripped apart with no prospect of it ever improving, so you can appreciate that a friend or family member who has lost a child is facing something so staggeringly large that they are lost, so now you can talk to them openly about their child, and be a true friend, not turning away or changing the subject. If they cry, then let them cry, it won't hurt you because after a few moments it will pass, and you can go back to your family with a fresh appreciation of just how lucky you are. Without a doubt, I'm jealous. Jealous that you have your family intact, that your child is growing when mine is forever 13.

This point in the book is the right place to thank those wonderful friends that I have mentioned previously. Take one part of the friends puzzle out and the lot collapses. Firstly, to Tim and Mary, who at the drop of a hat drove halfway across France to be with us in San Sebastian, to look after us for a week while we looked after Evie. They talked to us, but most importantly they listened and let us unload at the end of each painful day. Despite living in Southern France, we see and talk to them regularly, and I know that they will always be there if we need them. To Sam and Andy next door, for coordinating our neighbours to keep us fed for three and a half months, for sorting out the cats in the cattery when we returned to the UK, for feeding them for a month, but mostly for just being there, for talking to us, for listening, for being what a true friend should be, for never shying away from the hard parts, and lastly for just appearing every now and again for a coffee. To Karen, Garry, and David, three of Evie's godparents who have lost her too, have become Trustees at Evie's Gift, and yet remain staunchly loyal to us, who put up with our moods and the late changes that we inflict on them when we just can't face the world. To Sally and Leo for letting me teach a youngster to cook again, and watching over us at all times. To all of my trustees at Evie's Gift who have thrown themselves at the work to keep Evie's name and memory alive. And finally, to Sarah, Phil, and Izzy, without whom we would be in a far worse place. Your love, and that is the only word, has kept us going when we needed to find our way out of the darkness. You have kept us out of the abyss. You will never know how grateful we are to you as a family. But special mention must go to Izzy, Evie's best friend, who demonstrated to the whole world what true friendship really is. Izzy put aside her own pain again and again to be with Evie throughout her illness. She made Evie feel loved and cared about. She made Evie feel normal. For being the bravest young woman of all of Evie's friends, we will forever be in your debt because you kept Evie happy and that is the most precious gift.

It is also appropriate at this point to acknowledge the charities that have been involved in our lives. CLIC Sargent and Julia's House Hospice gave us incredible support when we were at home with Evie, as well as being with us still now that she has died. 'We Hear You', the cancer-related counselling charity which gave us access to counselling. But most of all thanks to The Compassionate Friends because without the support group and retreats I think we would now be buried in our duvet every day, unable to do very much at all. Being amongst likeminded people, people with the same pain, lifts an enormous weight from our shoulders. Wearing a mask all day is utterly exhausting, so being able to take it off every now and then when around other people is a massive help. We know that The Compassionate Friends will be there when no-one else can help. When no-one else understands that 20 years down the line Evie's death will be a distant memory for most, they will know that for us it is as fresh as the day that she died. A unique charity, run by unique people who share a common pain.

What happens now for Patsy and me is unknown. The future looks dark and foggy. But there will be moments of laughter, of remembering the better times too. We will quite literally make it up as we go along and that's fine. Staying flexible to change is key. Planning for the future is not only something that we find incredibly difficult, but also something that we don't want to do, because that action acknowledges that we are alone, without our beautiful girl. Some things are guaranteed. We will never forget Evie. I will never give up trying to find new ways to preserve her memory, her name. More friends will drift away; like it or not, that's the way of things, so we will just have to make new ones, most likely in our new bereaved parents' community. The charity we set up in her name will go on helping people. Evie's Gift only exists because she isn't here, so it is a way of getting her name out there for all to see. It is fitting, because even as a young girl she always helped others. And the pain, the anger, and frustration will also still be there. I doubt that these feelings will ever leave us, but that's just part of our new world.

I'm afraid that if you are looking for the uplifting ending to the book, full of optimism, then I can't provide it. I've always been an optimist, but even for me that is a step too far, and it wouldn't be true because that's not how I feel. Evie has been gone less than two years, so her loss is still pretty raw. Finding anything positive is difficult. But I also know that I can't give up on her, that I have to fight to change attitudes in a selfish society that is blind to this level of pain. I may not succeed. In fact, I will almost certainly fail, but I'm not going to be lying on my own death bed looking back thinking, "I wonder if I could have managed that or tried harder?" Evie changed my life in so many ways. She made me a better person because she forced me to think of someone else ahead of myself. I cannot betray that trust and love.

Evie, Mummy and I love you. We always will.

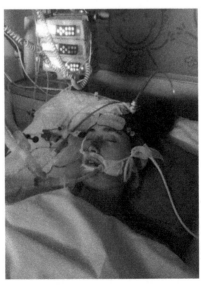

Lightning Source UK Ltd.
Milton Keynes UK
UKHW020627291219
355990UK00007B/42/P